# SPECIAL M[INISTER]
## of
# GOD'S WORD
# Certificate of Commissioning

**This is to Certify**

That_____

was commissioned a

# SPECIAL MINISTER
## of
# GOD'S WORD

according to the Rite of the Roman Catholic Church

on the_____ day of_____

in the year_____at_____

Let us pray to God our Father that

_____

chosen to proclaim the Word of God,
may be filled with His blessing

_____

Dated

_____

Pastor

*A Handbook for Lectors*

# Messengers
## *of*
# God's Word

Joseph M. Champlin

*Paulist Press* • *New York/Ramsey*

# ACKNOWLEDGEMENTS

Excerpts from the English translation of the *Lectionary for Mass* © 1969, International Committee on English in the Liturgy, Inc. (ICEL); excerpts from the English translation of the *Roman Calendar* © 1970, ICEL; excerpts from the English translation of *The Roman Missal* © 1973, ICEL. All rights reserved. Material from *Speech and Oral Reading Techniques for Mass Lectors and Commentators* by Benedict E. Hardman, published by The Liturgical Press, © by The Order of St. Benedict, Inc., Collegeville, Minnesota.

NIHIL OBSTAT
Rev. Richard M. Kopp

IMPRIMATUR
+Francis J. Harrison
*Bishop of Syracuse*

November 3, 1981

The *Nihil Obstat* and *Imprimatur* are official declarations that a book or pamphlet is free of doctrinal or moral error. No implication is contained therein that those who have granted the *Nihil Obstat* and *Imprimatur* agree with the contents, opinions or statements expressed.

Cover by *Tim McKeen.*
Interior and cover art by *Sr. Kristin Malone, S.S.J.*
Pronunciation Guide for Difficult Words (Appendix 1) by
*Robert Sadowski, C.S.P.*

Library of Congress Catalog Card Number: 82-60599

ISBN: 0-8091-2484-X

Published by Paulist Press,
545 Island Road, Ramsey, N.J. 07446

Printed and bound in the
United States of America

# Contents

# Introduction

When Mary Murphy proclaims the Scriptures at Blessed Sacrament Church in Alexandria, Virginia, people in the pews listen. They pay attention not because she is the local television announcer or a familiar radio broadcaster, but because this twelve year old girl reads extremely well.

She should. Mary comes from a tradition of lectors in the family and from a pattern at home which expects careful preparation prior to Sunday Mass.

Both the young lady's father and mother have served as readers for over a decade at Blessed Sacrament. As their three daughters, Clare 16, Kathleen 13 and Mary 12, finished confirmation classes, it was only natural for them to follow in the parents' footsteps. When that occurred either mom or dad or both would spend time training the newest candidate in the best techniques of oral reading. They also encouraged family members then and now to discuss the forthcoming scriptural passages at mealtime.

The training and encouragement shows. Parishioners see and hear the Word of God proclaimed by youthful lectors who know how to read with effectiveness in public and who speak these inspired words from their hearts.

This handbook is for people like the young and older Murphys, persons who have been designated and have accepted this ministry as messengers of God's Word. It covers the whys and hows behind lectors, why we have them in the liturgy and how they can function with even greater impact.

Chapters 1–2 examine the historical background and theological basis for readers in the Church today. The content may seem a bit heavy and technical, but that sets a solid base for what is to come.

Chapters 3–4 provide motivation for lectors, sketching in a general way some desirable inner qualities and seeing those ideals realized in the lives or at least hopes of actual readers in a parish.

Chapters 5–7 offer explanatory and resource material dealing with the lectionary, the liturgical year and the Mass itself. They give both an historical/theological overview of each and their very practical application to the reader's ministry. The last parts of these chapters contain information that has more immediate value when a particular season, situation or celebration arises. Consequently, lectors may wish to refer back to the pertinent chapters from time to time as occasions warrant.

Chapters 8–9 deal with the technical and spiritual preparation of a reader for his or her ministry. Chapter 8 includes a general principle of preparation and then ten specific do's and ten don'ts. Every now and then the lector may wish to read swiftly through these as a sort of a review or check-up. Chapter 9 contains a prayer for lectors and a series of ten spiritual renewal experiences. The reader might want to make a copy of the prayer for private use before proclamation preparation, Bible study or scriptural prayer. The ten renewal formulas would be helpful for a period or day of prayer, alone or with a group.

The appendix of words difficult to pronounce obviously can aid in the rehearsal process.

I would like here to extend my deep gratitude to: Mr. Donald F. Brophy, editor at the Paulist Press, who urged me to undertake this task of writing a handbook for lectors and whose confidence in my abilities has been very supportive; the parish lectors who contributed their personal testimonies in Chapter 4; Sister Charla Commins, C.S.J., Sister Lauren VanDermark, C.S.J., and Mr. Charles Calligaris for their helpful observations about the manuscript; Mrs. Patricia Gale who, as usual, transcribed swiftly and efficiently my increasingly illegible handwriting into clean typescript.

# Resurrecting an Ancient Ministry

After Jesus completed his forty days in the desert and successfully overcame a triple temptation by the devil, Luke's Gospel tells us that he returned "in the power of the Spirit to Galilee." There Christ taught in the synagogues and "all were loud in his praise."

This beginning of his public preaching ministry took place in the context of a Jewish synagogal service, an important point to keep in mind as we examine the historical background for the office or ministry of lector or reader.

Luke describes in detail what happened on one of those early occasions when Jesus spoke in the local synagogue:

> He came to Nazareth where he had been reared, and entering the synagogue on the sabbath as he was in the habit of doing, he stood up to do the reading.

> When the book of the prophet Isaiah was handed him, he unrolled the scroll and found the passage where it was written:

> "The spirit of the Lord is upon me;
> therefore he has anointed me.

He has sent me to bring glad tidings to the poor,
    to proclaim liberty to captives,
Recovery of sight to the blind
    and release to prisoners,
To announce a year of favor from the Lord."

Rolling up the scroll he gave it back to the assistant and sat down. All in the synagogue had their eyes fixed on him.

Then he began by saying to them, "Today this Scripture passage is fulfilled in your hearing." All who were present spoke favorably of him; they marveled at the appealing discourse which came from his lips. They also asked, "Is not this Joseph's son?"[1]

Religious life in Palestine centered around the synagogue. There was but one temple, that at Jerusalem, and the only sacrifices offered by the Jews took place in this magnificent structure. However, wherever ten Jewish families could be found the law required a synagogue, a building designed for teaching, just as the temple had been constructed for sacrifice. Since the population of Nazareth may have exceeded twenty thousand, that town or city undoubtedly possessed several synagogues.[2]

Believers regularly assembled in the synagogue and particularly, of course, on the sabbath. The service normally included an opening worship section for prayer, a part for reading of the Scriptures and a teaching period similar to our homily or sermon.

The assistant or *chazzan* mentioned in the incident had several responsibilities: he kept the building clean, announced the coming of the sabbath with three blasts of the silver trumpet from the synagogue roof, taught in the village school and, since the Scriptures were written not in books but on rolls, took them out, presented them to the readers and, later, returned the scrolls to their storage spots.[3]

The biblical section included two scriptural passages, an excerpt from the "Law" and another from the "Prophets."

The "Law" portion came first and carried over from one meeting to the next in rather continuous fashion such that the whole text was completed during a stipulated period and then the series began all over again. The "Prophets" portion was chosen at will.

These readings were not done by a single reader, but distributed among several, usually at least seven, each of whom read a verse or a number of verses.[4]

During the course of the service no professional minister or specified individual gave the address. Instead, the president of the assembly invited any distinguished person present to comment, with an open discussion to follow. The speaker sat down to deliver his message, following the pattern of the teaching rabbis and reminding us of our English term, a professor's "chair."[5]

With that background in mind, the reader might return to Luke's account above and go through this passage again, noticing how Jesus' actions would have naturally developed out of the customs in those days. In addition, we might begin to compare what Jesus and the synagogue service did then and what we do now in the Mass.

Our understanding of the first Eucharists and the very early format of Christian liturgies is naturally vague and sketchy. After the initial Last Supper, celebrated at night within the context of the paschal or passover ritual banquet (1 Corinthians 11:17–24), it appears that for a while the Eucharist generally continued to be offered in connection with a meal, which, according to both Jewish and Hellenistic or Greek custom, occurred during the evening hour. Eventually the ordinary meal and the sacred banquet were separated, a division that opened up the possibility of offering Mass at other times. Since Sunday, the day of Jesus' resurrection, was very early on urged as the day to celebrate the Eucharist and since Christ had risen in the morning before sunrise, the next step transferred all the services to the morning hours.[6]

During the first decades after Jesus' resurrection Christians gathered for their own eucharistic celebrations, but normally likewise attended the synagogue services on the sabbath and even daily. The Acts of the Apostles tells us: "They went to the temple area together each day, while in their homes they broke bread."[7]

However, after a persecution in the year 44, more and more of them broke with the synagogue, and their hour of worship devoted to reading took on a more specifically Christian shape. Gradually combined with the Eucharist, it became a fore-Mass or, in today's terms, the liturgy of the Word.[8]

Nevertheless, their Jewish roots and deep exposure to the synagogue service led Christians to maintain much of its style and structure in their own worship. We see that in the first full account of a Christian Mass celebration, a description preserved for us from a work of St. Justin, the philosopher and martyr, who wrote his *First Apology* in Rome about 150:

> And on that day which is called after the sun, all who are in the towns and in the country gather together for a communal celebration. And then the memoirs of the Apostles or the writings of the Prophets are read, as long as time permits. After the reader has finished his task, the one presiding gives an address, urgently admonishing his hearers to practice these beautiful teachings in their lives. Then all stand up together and recite prayers.

> After the end of the prayers, as has already been re-
> marked above, the bread and wine mixed with water are
> brought, and the president offers up prayers and thanks-
> givings, as much as in him lies. The people chime in with
> an Amen. Then takes place the distribution, to all attend-
> ing, of the things over which the thanksgiving had been
> spoken, and the deacons bring a portion to the absent.
> Besides, those who are well-to-do give whatever they
> will. What is gathered is deposited with the one presid-
> ing, who therewith helps orphans and widows. . . .[9]

In that excerpt, note that the reader is a distinct person
from the "one presiding," or the "president" who would
have been a bishop or a priest.

Both the synagogue service and the earliest Christian liturgies included, then, lectors, persons who proclaimed the
biblical text. These individuals were always someone other
than the leader of the worship, a procedure which reflected a
certain dramatic tone: the Word coming from God is spoken
by a different person than the word rising from the Church
to God.[10]

The dignity of this task—to utter the inspired passages
for all to hear—naturally required that readers reflect exem-
plary Christian conduct and receive a certain amount of education. As a consequence they came rather quickly to be
subjected to the discipline and control of Church authorities.
The office of lector as a special position, the oldest of the
lesser degrees of ordination, appears already in the second
century.[11]

Tertullian (160–230), for example, is the first writer to
mention the presence of an officially recognized lector or
reader in the community. Later, Pope St. Cornelius (c. 250)
wrote a letter to his friend Fabius and enumerated the clergy
of Rome: one bishop; forty-six priests (presbyters); seven

deacons; seven subdeacons; forty-two acolytes; fifty-two exorcists, readers and Church maintenance personnel.[12]

While the function of the lector or reader shifted greatly with the passage of time, mention of them even in a so-called private Mass is made as late as the thirteenth century. Moreover, the Roman Missal published in 1570 and used exclusively until the revised Order of Mass was issued by Pope Paul VI urges that the epistle be sung not by the celebrant but by a lector in surplice.[13]

In the beginning the lector, an accomplished person, not only read the Scriptures at liturgies, but also could serve as a teacher, instructing the faithful in the knowledge of the biblical texts.[14]

Very early in the Church's history, however, perhaps during the fourth or fifth century or even before, a movement developed restricting the reader's function and bringing it under authoritative control. While an individual's natural gift for proclamation and personal desire to do so were still considered, the critically important step was to be commissioned for the task in some way. That bestowed the distinguishing mark of the Church and the stamp of its authority or approval. While the reader, of course, did not receive ordination of the higher kinds, the ministry of lector did come more and more under tight regulation through official designation. Eventually and rather naturally those in the loftier orders began to absorb the lector's tasks.

Consequently, the reader's role first was reduced to proclamation at worship. Moreover, in time nearly all of the lector's liturgical functions were absorbed by those in higher orders—the deacon caring for the Gospel, a subdeacon the epistle. Probably because lectors no longer exercised any function, the office disappeared from many listings in documents between 251 and 900.[15]

Ultimately, the position of lector became in practice

merely a seldom used minor order, one of four required for a man on his way to the priesthood, which meant little outside the seminary and not much more within the walls of that institution.

Around the Council of Trent in the sixteenth century some proposed making clerics with these lesser orders of acolyte or reader more active in liturgical celebrations. Moreover, a few even recommended that when no cleric was available suitable laymen could fulfill this role. But the Council fathers were not ready for this step and the proposal died.[16]

Just prior to the Second Vatican Council the Roman Catholic Mass was generally a one-man, one-book service. The missal contained in Latin all the prayers and readings; the priest celebrant said and did almost everything.

However, the climate had changed since those days of Trent four hundred years earlier. There was a movement both official from above and grass roots from below to revise the liturgy and to involve lay persons more actively in the sacred mysteries of our Church.

Those efforts bore fruit with the gradual reintroduction of laity, now including women, as readers of God's Word during worship services. That resurrection of an ancient ministry, the lector, became formalized in the General Instruction of the Roman Missal as we will see with some detail in the next chapter. The following excerpt from section 66, nevertheless, reflects how clearly the reformed rite returns to a practice common in the very earliest days of Christianity: "The reader, although a layman, has his own proper function in the eucharistic celebration and should exercise this even though ministers of a higher rank are present."[17]

In 1972, Pope Paul VI issued a document on the question of minor orders, including that of lector. The text, entitled *Ministeria quaedam* from two of the Latin words in its

11

opening sentence, made some significant changes and brought the situation more in tune with current reality. Among those modifications were:

- What once were called minor orders now are termed "ministries."

- The offices of subdeacon, porter and exorcist have been eliminated.

- The ministries of reader and acolyte are preserved.

- What was formerly done by the subdeacon is now done by the reader and acolyte.

- These two and other ministries may be committed to lay Christians.

- Readers and acolytes are no longer "ordained" but "instituted" for these ministries.

- Candidates for diaconate and priesthood are to receive the ministries of reader and acolyte, unless they have already done so, and are to exercise them for a fitting time, in order to be better disposed for the future service of the word and of the altar.

- Institution in these two ministries is reserved to men.[18]

The last restriction, in addition to other factors, has reduced the impact of the Vatican document on the Church in the United States. Nearly every parish has a few, perhaps many women readers, a function approved for them by other official decrees and ritual books from the Holy See. Moreover, the role of acolyte or server still continues to be fulfilled mostly by young boys. To install only adult men, other than those on the way to the diaconate or priesthood, in these two ministries which are at the same time actually being carried out by others not legally qualified to be official acolytes or lectors seems inappropriate.

As a consequence, one seldom meets a formally installed reader or acolyte, yet lay persons performing these and other ministries in and outside the liturgy continue to multiply, and various home-grown installation, commissioning or blessing ceremonies occur on both the diocesan and parish level.[19]

Nevertheless, the Vatican text does clarify the role of reader, lends it support and insures that the position of lector as a function separate from the president or priest celebrant, thus described in St. Justin the Martyr's account, will be retained. Moreover, this decree specifies a reader's tasks and offers a few recommendations for the proper fulfillment of those responsibilities.

But more of that in the next and succeeding chapters.

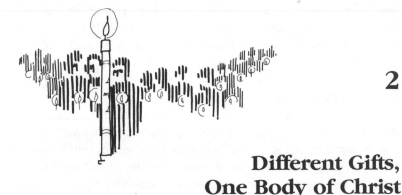

# Different Gifts,
# One Body of Christ

Last Holy Saturday a near capacity crowd assembled in our parish church for the 7:30 P.M. Easter vigil service. Each person who entered received a taper which eventually was lighted from the flame of a huge paschal candle carried down the main aisle of the darkened structure by the priest/deacon.

After the proclamation of the Exultet or Easter song of praise, participants extinguished their candles and sat down to hear the Word of God. A young married couple, parents of two small children, came forward and, in dialogue fashion, read the Genesis account of creation. A high school girl followed them to the lectern and proclaimed the story of God's chosen people and their deliverance from slavery through the waters of the Red Sea as described in Exodus. Later, a recently confirmed eighth grade boy raised the community's vision by reading a portion of St. Paul's Letter to the Romans.

That night a married man in his thirties made a profession of faith and entered the Church, receiving confirmation in the process and, with his family, bringing forward the gifts for the eucharistic liturgy. Just prior to his presentation procession, another father about his age, whose son soon would receive First Holy Communion, spoke the petitions for the Prayer of the Faithful or General Intercessions.

At Communion time eight lay persons assisted with cups of our Lord's Precious Blood, thus offering all present an opportunity to receive under both kinds should they so choose.

Such a fully participated Easter vigil celebration was hardly an exceptional event among Catholic churches in the United States. In fact, it would more represent today's standard procedure, the normative liturgy for most American parishes.

Yet this active involvement of each person in the worshiping community and the employment of so many lay people in leadership or ministry roles during the liturgy do reflect radical departures from the pre-Second Vatican Council approach.

In those days, that parallel service usually took place very early Holy Saturday morning, consumed about three hours, was totally in Latin, attracted very few, only the most devoted people, and actively engaged practically no lay persons as lead ministers like readers, eucharistic distributors or gift bearers. The laity remained pretty much interested but passive participants, marveling but generally mute spectators whose sole direct involvement came at Communion time.

Our present post-Vatican II style, however, includes more than a reordering of externals; it embraces a change in theory, a shift in theological emphasis. That change or shift recognizes the basic baptismal dignity, diverse gifts and rightful, active part in the Church's life and worship of every Christian.

The seeds of this shift occurred long before the Second Vatican Council convened in the early 1960's. During the final decades of the last century and throughout the 1900's, those promoting the liturgical movement from above or below urged more lay involvement in worship and supported their practical recommendations by sound theological arguments and careful historical research.

Pope Pius XII gave that basis in good theology a strong boost in 1943 when he issued his encyclical on the Mystical Body of Christ. This document examined St. Paul's teaching, especially in his Letters to the Corinthians, that the Church is the body of Christ, with Jesus as the head and we the members: "As all the members of the human body, though they are many, form one body, so also are the faithful in Christ."[1]

Not only does this mean that there exists a wonderful, real, mysterious union among all the members and with the Lord, it also implies that each part or person has a special role to play for the health and success of the total body. "In the building up of Christ's body there is engaged a diversity of members and functions. There is only one Spirit who, according to his own richness and the needs of the ministries, gives his different gifts for the welfare of the Church."[2]

The liturgy, finally, according to this encyclical, becomes the official prayer or external expression of that living body, that mystical union of Christ and us that we call the Church. Each member consequently contributes to the success of the body's worship.

The Vatican Council fathers took this notion of the Mystical Body of Christ and developed a newer concept of the Church as the "people of God," a notion with slightly different nuances. In their Dogmatic Constitution on the Church they wrote:

> Christ instituted this new covenant, namely the new covenant in his blood; he called a race made up of Jews and Gentiles which would be one, not according to the flesh,

16

but in the Spirit, and this race would be the new people of God. For those who believe in Christ, who are re-born, not from a corruptible seed, but from an incorruptible one through the Word of the living God, not from flesh, but from water and the Holy Spirit, are finally established as a chosen race, a royal priesthood, a holy nation . . . who in times past were not a people, but now are the people of God.[3]

Baptism and confirmation make us members of that body, the holy people of God. As members we assume both rights and privileges as well as duties and responsibilities.

In 1980 the American bishops reflected on the fifteenth anniversary of Vatican II's Decree on the Apostolate of the Laity with a statement entitled "Called and Gifted: The American Catholic Laity." They reinforced in it this idea about the relationship between baptism/confirmation and the people of God: "Baptism and confirmation empower all believers to share in some form of ministry. Although the specific form of participation in ministry varies according to the gifts of the Holy Spirit, all who share in this work are united with one another."[4]

Our bishops expanded upon this point and noted that just as ordination gives bishops, priests and deacons authority of leadership to serve God's people, so the initiation sacraments empower lay women and men with the right and responsibility to participate in the Church's mission. Lay persons possess a unique competency in certain areas of life because of their particular talents, education and experience. They extend the Church's presence in the world. The bishops see no conflict or divisiveness necessary because of this fresh recognition of the laity's important position. Instead they affirm the trend.[5]

The Council fathers had taught precisely these truths

during the previous decade when they examined the nature of the Church and related those concepts to worship and the liturgy:

> Incorporated into the Church by baptism, the faithful are appointed by their baptismal character to Christian religious worship; reborn as sons of God, they must profess before men the faith they have received from God through the Church. By the sacrament of confirmation they are more perfectly bound to the Church and are endowed with the special strength of the Holy Spirit. Hence they are, as true witnesses of Christ, more strictly obliged to spread the faith by word and deed.[6]

In another place, the bishops at Vatican II remind us that the liturgy also provides lay persons with the energy and strength to carry out this work as apostles: "Nourished by their active participation in the liturgical life of their community, they engage zealously in its apostolic works."[7]

Our former apostolic delegate, Archbishop Jean Jadot, speaking at "Growing Together," a conference on shared ministry, stressed that involvement of lay persons in the life of the Church as readers, leaders of song, eucharistic distributors, etc., is critical for the United States. Their importance, however, arises not merely from a need created by the decline in available clergy, but because of the unique gifts they possess and can contribute to the building up of the Church.[8]

The bishops at the Second Vatican Council underscored that same teaching about special talents of lay persons and their value for the Church:

> The Holy Spirit makes holy the people, leads them and enriches them with his virtues. Allotting his gifts according as he wills, he also distributes special graces among the faithful of every rank. By these gifts he makes them

fit and ready to undertake various tasks and offices for
the renewal and building up of the Church, as it is written, "The manifestation of the Spirit is given to everyone for profit." Whether these charisms be very
remarkable or more simple and widely diffused, they are
to be received with thanksgiving and consolation since
they are fitting and useful for the needs of the Church.[9]

This diversity of individual gifts combining to serve one
purpose, one body, one people of God, has been compared
to a symphony orchestra and the parish leader to the music
conductor. Each musician, each instrument has a beauty and
power by itself, but linked together they produce a different,
perhaps more beautiful and certainly more powerful sound.
That analogy rather nicely comes alive through the instance
of the Holy Saturday Easter vigil celebration held in our
church which we described at the start of this chapter.[10]

Using those various gifts for the building up of the
Church is to carry on the mission and the ministry of Jesus,
to share with the Lord his task of bringing about here and
now the kingdom of God.

Benedictine Archbishop Rembert G. Weakland of Mil-
waukee, speaking at that conference on "Growing Together" cited earlier, quite nicely pulled together all these
thoughts on the people of God, our call from baptism and
confirmation, the uniqueness of individual gifts and one's
ministry which flows from these talents and vocation. He
mentioned the term "shared responsibility" and recalled the
old adage that when many share responsibility, no one has
the responsibility. But with a correct concept of the Church,
however, we see that each in fact has a responsibility for
building up the kingdom, but according to his or her own
specialized calling.

This means a unity in the midst of diversity, a blending

together in a delicate, beautiful and balanced way personal gifts and the needs of the whole community. It requires prayer, humility and the presence of the Spirit to bring about that balance and unity.[11]

These theological truths have been applied by official Church documents very practically to the liturgy in general and to the ministry of lector or reader in particular.

The Constitution on the Sacred Liturgy, with a truly pivotal paragraph, established as a basic principle in reforming our worship active involvement of and full participation by lay persons.

> Mother Church earnestly desires that all the faithful should be led to that full, conscious, and active participation in liturgical celebrations which is demanded by the very nature of the liturgy, and to which the Christian people, "a chosen race, a royal priesthood, a holy nation, a redeemed people" (1 Pet 2:9, 4–5) have a right and obligation by reason of their baptism.
>
> In the restoration and promotion of the sacred liturgy the full and active participation by all the people is the aim to be considered before all else, for it is the primary and indispensable source from which the faithful are to derive the true Christian spirit.[12]

That decree in a subsequent section more specifically outlined how this participation would be achieved, actually mentioning readers as exercising a genuine liturgical function and briefly describing the manner in which such tasks should be carried out.

> In liturgical celebrations each person, minister, or layman who has an office to perform should carry out all

and only those parts which pertain to his office by the nature of the rite and the norms of the liturgy.

Servers, readers, commentators, and members of the choir also exercise a genuine liturgical function. They ought, therefore, to discharge their offices with the sincere piety and decorum demanded by so exalted a ministry and rightly expected of them by God's people.

Consequently they must all be deeply imbued with the spirit of the liturgy, each in his own measure, and they must be trained to perform their functions in a correct and orderly manner.[13]

When the revised Roman Missal appeared nearly a decade later, its General Instruction clearly reflected those guiding norms for participation by many with diverse functions in the liturgy. In Chapter III, "Offices and Ministries in the Mass," it even cites or rephrases the articles we have just quoted.

Everyone in the eucharistic assembly has the right and duty to take his own part according to the diversity of orders and functions. In exercising his function, everyone, whether minister or layman, should do that and only that which belongs to him, so that in the liturgy the Church may be seen in its variety of orders and ministries.[14]

An earlier paragraph in that General Instruction indicates who is to proclaim what reading:

In the readings the treasures of the Bible are opened to the people; this is the table of God's word. Reading the Scriptures is traditionally considered a ministerial, not a presidential, function. It is desirable that the Gospel be read by a deacon or, in his absence, by a priest other than the one presiding; the other readings are proclaimed by a reader. In the absence of a deacon or another priest, the celebrant reads the Gospel.[15]

Under a division on "Special Ministries," the Roman Missal, finally, outlines in some detail the duties and qualifications of a reader, including mention of the appropriateness of women as lectors, subject to the judgment of the body of bishops in a particular area.

The reader is instituted to proclaim the Scripture readings, with the exception of the Gospel. He may also announce the intentions of the general intercessions and, in the absence of a cantor of the psalm, sing or read the psalm between the readings.

The reader, although a layman, has his own proper function in the eucharistic celebration and should exercise this even though ministers of a higher rank are present.

It is necessary that those who exercise the ministry of reading, even if they have not received institution, be qualified and carefully prepared so that the reading should develop in the faithful a profound appreciation of Scripture.

The conference of bishops may permit a woman to proclaim the readings prior to the Gospel and to announce the intentions of the general intercessions.

Laymen, even if they have not received institution as ministers, may perform all the functions below those re-

served to deacons. Services performed outside the pres-
byterium may also be given to women at the discretion
of the rector of the church.

If there are several persons present who can exercise the
same ministry, different parts of it may be assigned to
them. For example, one deacon may take the sung parts,
another serve at the altar. If there are several readings, it
is better to distribute them among a number of readers,
and likewise with other functions.[16]

The American bishops have so authorized women to
serve as lectors.

In the last chapter we referred to the Vatican decree on
certain ministries in the Church. Published after the Roman
Missal, it includes a description of the reader which, while
repetitious of some elements in documents already noted,
contains additional insights.

The reader is appointed for a function proper to him,
that of reading the Word of God in the liturgical assembly. Accordingly, he is to read the lessons from Sacred
Scripture, except for the Gospel, in the Mass and other
sacred celebrations; he is to recite the psalm between the
readings when there is no psalmist; he is to present the
intentions for the general intercessions in the absence of
a deacon or cantor; he is to direct the singing and the
participation by the faithful; he is to instruct the faithful
for the worthy reception of the sacraments. He may also,
insofar as necessary, take care of preparing other faithful
who by a temporary appointment are to read the Scriptures in liturgical celebrations. That he may more fittingly and perfectly fulfill these functions, let him meditate
assiduously on Sacred Scripture.

Let the reader be aware of the office he has undertaken and make every effort and employ suitable means to acquire that increasingly warm and living love and knowledge of the Scriptures that will make him a more perfect disciple of the Lord.[17]

Persons who function as readers have been summoned to holiness, to be more perfect disciples of the Lord, to discharge their offices with sincere piety and decorum. We will now examine those ideals and seek to identify some inner qualities that a lector should possess or at least strive to achieve.

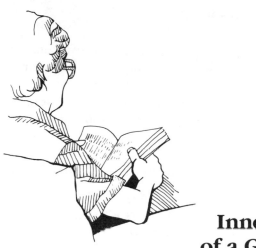

# 3

# Inner Qualities
# of a Good Lector

Dr. Elisabeth Kübler-Ross, a psychiatrist who directs the Family Service and Mental Health Center of South Cook County in Chicago, has become famous as the expert on death and dying. In an interview some years ago, she stressed the need for certain appropriate inner qualities for ministers to the seriously ill. Whether Protestant clergyperson, Catholic priest, Jewish rabbi, professional health care worker or volunteer lay visitor, Kübler-Ross insisted that these people must have inside themselves a certain comfortableness about the subject of death and a faith in the immortality of the human spirit.

Unless those interior attitudes are present, she maintained, the person calling upon a desperately ill patient could hinder, even hurt more than help. Moreover, the Chicago psychiatrist noted that the presence or absence of such inner qualities would be communicated to the sick people without a word being said. A patient intuits, senses, knows when they are there and, unfortunately, when they are not there.

In parallel fashion, the appropriate interior qualities of

the reader likewise become apparent to listeners almost without a single word being proclaimed. The community gathered for worship simply senses that he or she believes, loves Sacred Scripture, prays, prepares conscientiously and has a humble, yet confident awareness of the lector's dignity. The congregation also silently recognizes the lack of those essential characteristics.

We will now look at each of these qualities in some detail.

### FAITH IN CHRIST'S PRESENCE THROUGH THE INSPIRED WORD

A woman in Delaware coordinates as a part-time volunteer the lectors in her parish, but works full-time in industry as an executive sales manager. She commented: "I am good in my job because I believe in my product. So, too, readers will be good in this ministry if they believe in their product—the Word of God."

Liturgical pioneer and respected scholar Benedictine Father Godfrey Dickmann maintains that the doctrinal basis for all of the ritual reforms directed by the Second Vatican Council can be found in paragraph seven of the *Constitution on the Sacred Liturgy.* That section highlights in staccato fashion the many presences of Christ in the liturgy:

> To accomplish so great a work Christ is always present in his Church, especially in its liturgical celebrations. He is present in the Sacrifice of the Mass not only in the person of his minister, "the same now offering, through the ministry of priests, who formerly offered himself on the cross," but especially in the eucharistic species. By his power he is present in the sacraments so that when anybody baptizes it is really Christ himself who baptizes. He is present in his Word since it is he himself who speaks

when the Holy Scriptures are read in the Church. Lastly, he is present when the Church prays and sings, for he has promised: "Where two or three are gathered together in my name there am I in the midst of them" (Mt. 18:20).[1]

This presence of Christ in the Word is reiterated in a later section of the same document which speaks about the educational nature of the liturgy. "Although the sacred liturgy is principally the worship of the divine majesty it likewise contains much instruction for the people. For in the liturgy God speaks to his people, and Christ is still proclaiming his Gospel."[2]

When the Church some years later published the reformed Roman Missal, it naturally followed the principles enunciated by the Council fathers. The General Instruction for the new Order of Mass thus describes the structure of a eucharistic liturgy, the place of biblical readings in it and the presence of Christ in those scriptural passages.

> Although the Mass is made up of the liturgy of the Word and the liturgy of the Eucharist, the two parts are so closely connected as to form one act of worship. The table of God's Word and of Christ's body is prepared and from it the faithful are instructed and nourished.[3]

> When the Scriptures are read in the Church, God himself speaks to his people, and it is Christ, present in his Word, who proclaims the Gospel. The readings should be listened to with respect; they are a principal element of the liturgy. In the biblical readings God's Word is addressed to all men of every era and is understandable in itself, but a homily, as a living explanation of the Word, increases its effectiveness and is an integral part of the service.[4]

Readings from Scripture and the chants between the readings form the main part of the liturgy of the Word. The homily, profession of faith, and general intercessions or prayer of the faithful develop and complete it. In the readings, explained by the homily, God speaks to his people of redemption and salvation and nourishes their spirit; Christ is present among the faithful through his Word. Through the chants the people make God's Word their own and express their adherence to it through the profession of faith. Finally, moved by this Word, they pray in the general intercessions for the needs of the Church and for the world's salvation.[5]

In the readings the treasures of the Bible are opened to the people: this is the table of God's Word.[6]

The liturgy teaches that the reading of the Gospel should be done with great reverence; it is distinguished from the other readings by special marks of honor. A special minister is appointed to proclaim it, preparing himself by a blessing or prayer. By standing to hear the reading and by their acclamations, the people recognize and acknowledge that Christ is present and speaking to them. Marks of reverence are also given to the book of Gospels itself.[7]

A faith that recognizes Christ truly is present and speaking to us in the biblical text we hear or proclaim stands as the first, fundamental and most essential inner quality of a lector. The second flows from it.

### A WARM AND LIVING LOVE FOR THE SCRIPTURES

Holy Sepulcher Church in Butler, Pennsylvania dramatizes the importance of the Scriptures during Mass and focuses attention on the reader by having two processional candles on either side of the lectern throughout the liturgy of the Word. Servers move those to the altar for the liturgy of the Eucharist.

In Lowellville, Ohio those who enter the handsome Most Holy Rosary Church in that Youngstown suburb will immediately discover in the vestibule an open Bible with a spotlight centering our interest there.

If we believe that Christ is present in the Scriptures, then those inspired words should logically become the light of our lives and the center of our heart's concern.

The bishops at Vatican II listed as one of the general principles governing the liturgical reform an emphasis on and promotion of Sacred Scripture. They in that section also urged a "sweet and living love" for the Bible.

> Sacred Scripture is of the greatest importance in the cele-
> bration of the liturgy. For it is from it that lessons are
> read and explained in the homily, and psalms are sung. It
> is from the Scriptures that the prayers, collects, and
> hymns draw their inspiration and their force, and that ac-
> tions and signs derive their meaning. Hence in order to
> achieve the restoration, progress, and adaptation of the
> sacred liturgy it is essential to promote the sweet and liv-
> ing love for Sacred Scripture to which the venerable tra-
> dition of Eastern and Western rites gives testimony.[8]

When Pope Paul VI decreed the institution of readers, he urged anyone holding that office to "make every effort and employ suitable means to acquire that increasingly warm and living love and knowledge of the Scriptures that will make him a more perfect disciple of the Lord."[9]

At the Second Vatican Council, the fathers issued among its many documents the *Dogmatic Constitution on Divine*

*Revelation.* Section 25 of that text likewise urges this love for the Scriptures, explains why, and tells how the reverence for the Word should be preserved or fostered. It urges both clergy and lay persons to immerse themselves in the inspired books by regular sacred reading and diligent study. Recalling the ancient motto, "Ignorance of the Scriptures is ignorance of Christ," the Constitution recommends that we seek out this revealed Word in the official liturgy, in private reflective reading and in those Bible services which, at that time, were just beginning to spread rapidly everywhere.

The bishops reminded all that there should be a certain dialogue in prayerful reading of Sacred Scripture. We thus speak to God as we pray and listen to the Lord as we read the divinely given Word.

Finally, the text urges local bishops to provide suitable translations and proper commentaries so that all members of the Church can safely and profitably read the Scriptures and "become steeped in their spirit."[10]

When we love someone we want to be with that person as much as possible; we think about the individual continually and we can never know enough about him or her. Similarly, if we have a warm, living love for the Scriptures, it follows that we will wish to be with, ponder and peruse the sacred books.

## A HUNGER FOR PRAYERFUL READING, REFLECTION AND STUDY OF THE BIBLE

When the bishop celebrates the official institution of readers or when a pastor formally designates certain individuals for temporary service as lectors, the ritual recommends an instruction to the candidates and even provides a model exhortation. The concluding paragraph places a serious responsibility upon the future readers:

When you proclaim God's Word to others, see that you are ready to accept it yourselves in obedience to the Holy Spirit. Meditate on God's Word often, so that you will daily grow in God's love and by your way of life show forth to the world our Savior Jesus Christ.[11]

Moments later in a prayer or blessing prior to the actual handing over of a Bible and the words of institution, the bishop or pastor who adapts this ritual to his parish use prays:

As they meditate on your word,
help them to understand it better
and to proclaim it faithfully to your people.[12]

Pope Paul VI, in his description of the reader's role, added this requisite for a faithful discharge of the lector's duties: "That he may more fittingly and perfectly fulfill these functions, let him meditate assiduously on Sacred Scripture."[13]

Scripture scholar Geoffrey E. Wood urges students of the Bible to make the passage personal, to interiorize the scriptural text. "To experience the Scriptures—and to stimulate their experience by the congregation—you must read the Scriptures from inside. You must get into the piece you read, into the author, into the scene. . . . You must assimilate the passage or be absorbed by it. . . . Immersing yourself in that passage means identifying with everything in it."[14]

That kind of interiorizing or personalizing the biblical text can be achieved in a simple way by slowly, prayerfully reading a passage and then reflecting on what God is saying to me, what comments the Lord is making about my life, and what the Spirit is doing to me now through this incident or excerpt.

Such personalization, nevertheless, will be even more productive if we prepare for the reflective period by some study of the text under consideration.

I would like to illustrate both the simpler approach and the more studious one through an incident in which Jesus, asleep in a boat with the apostles, was awakened and miraculously calmed the wind and stilled the Sea of Galilee. Readers anxious to move on with this book may wish to skip over the next few paragraphs; those eager to experience these principles in action now might first secure their Bible or at least a New Testament.

That calming of the storm occurs in each of the Synoptic Gospels: Matthew 8:23–27; Mark 4:35–41; Luke 8:22–25.

For the simpler approach, first locate one of the accounts; then place yourself in the presence of God and be conscious that the Bible in your hands is a special book containing the Lord's own words. Next, read the passage slowly, prayerfully, carefully. When finished ask yourself: How does this incident apply to me? What are the inner storms of my life which need to be stilled or calmed? Those personal feelings of insecurity which make me fearful and unsure? The push of my passions which seem like a turbulent sea within me? The worries about my future—the dread of death, the concern about cancer, the fret over jobs and finances. The resentment which lingers from past hurts?

Finally, recognize that the Jesus who calmed the wind and stilled the sea can and does wish here and now through this word to calm and still those violent, upsetting waves within you.

The second, more studious method observes all the above steps, but precedes the prayerful reading and reflection with a bit of study, a research limited only by time and available resource texts.

For example, any substantial version of the Bible will contain footnotes that cross-reference scriptural texts. Hence, if you start with Matthew's version of the storm on the lake, a footnote will tell you that parallel accounts can be found in Mark and Luke. To read all three reveals interesting details and insights. Thus in this event, Mark shows Jesus "in the stern, asleep on the cushion" and actually saying to the sea, "Peace, be still." Neither of those points occurs in the other descriptions.

Using biblical commentaries likewise enriches this kind of prayerful study. William Barclay's *The Daily Study Bible Series* is a popular multi-volume paperback commentary on the New Testament. That Scripture scholar's writings contain an enormous amount of information about the cultural and religious scene at the time of Jesus. Such background makes any incident come alive and sheds additional light on the Lord's words or actions.

Following through with our illustration, Barclay has two pages on Matthew 8:23–27 which describe the physical setting of the event, provide comments from observers on how rapidly and violently storms arise there, and explain two Greek words that delineate the storm itself and the kind of waves swamping the boat.[15]

Roman Catholic charismatic Scripture teacher George Martin has written an excellent paperback, *Reading Scripture as the Word of God: Practical Approaches and Attitudes*,[16] that would be extremely helpful for the lector who heretofore has not read the Bible frequently or regularly. His observations on reading, understanding, listening and praying Scripture are down-to-earth and helpful, wise and inspirational. "To enter into this mystery of God's Word, your lifetime of listening to the Word of God can begin, today, with a fifteen-minute reading."[17]

The Council Fathers also gave their support to a pattern of regular biblical reading and meditation:

> Only the light of faith and meditation on the Word of God can enable us to find everywhere and always the God "in whom we live and exist" (Acts 17:28); only thus can we seek his will in everything, see Christ in all men, acquaintance or stranger, and make sound judgments on the true meaning and value of temporal realities both in themselves and in relation to man's end.[18]

Father Gerard Sloyan, Scripture scholar, theologian, and liturgist, has listed twenty-four pragmatic "Touchstones for Readers." Number one is "Read the Bible privately on a regular basis." Number 16 is "Read the Bible privately on a regular basis." Number 25 is "Read the Bible privately on a regular basis."[19]

## CONSCIENTIOUS IN PREPARATION

On a recent cross-country flight I was listening to a program of music by Ella Fitzgerald and Frank Sinatra. The announcer mentioned before one of Sinatra's sets that this artist prepared for each recording of an album as if it were to be his last. He physically trained for the performance by restricting his eating, drinking, and smoking habits as well as, of course, getting musically keyed for the occasion.

My brother, arts and entertainment editor of the Los Angeles *Times,* covered the singer's supposedly last appearance some years ago in Las Vegas. Sinatra rehearsed with Harry James and his band for days in advance, flew to Las Vegas the morning of the show and practiced for two more hours. Then, at 5:00 P.M., on his own, he called another rehearsal.

The audience would not have judged from his seemingly informal, unrehearsed, casual manner that night just how carefully Sinatra worked in advance on every detail.

And this for a perishable crown.

We would not expect Richard Burton to step on stage without having looked at his lines.

The story is told of a famous Irish actor who was in town for the weekend. He stopped at the parish house and offered to proclaim the readings that Sunday. The pastor agreed. Early Saturday morning he called at the rectory and sought to have the church opened. The somewhat disheveled and disturbed priest responded, "No, not today; tomorrow it is you will be reading."

"I know, Father, but I am here to rehearse."

And he did so for an hour.

The Council of fathers would agree with that conscientious approach. They urged readers, along with other liturgical ministers, "to discharge their offices with the sincere piety and decorum demanded by so exalted a ministry and rightly expected of them by God's people. Consequently they must all be deeply imbued with the Spirit of the liturgy, each in his own measure, and they must be trained to perform their functions in a correct and orderly manner."[20]

At the ceremony of institution, the bishop invites all present to pray that "God our Father will bless these servants who are chosen for the ministry of readers, so that [they will] carefully perform the task entrusted to them...."[21]

Pope John Paul II likewise urged that the Scripture passages should be entrusted "to a reader who has been instituted as such or to other spiritually and technically trained lay people."[22]

It seems clear that racing into the sacristy five minutes before Mass to grab the missalette and glance through the readings hardly fits the ideal of conscientious preparation.

## HUMILITY AND CONFIDENCE

Lectors need to combine within themselves a sense of awe, awareness of the reader's dignity and importance, and trust, conscious that this is God's Word and work, not ours.

"Apart from me you can do nothing."[23]

"In him who is the source of my strength I have strength for everything."[24]

In 1964, the Bishops' Commission on the Liturgical Apostolate published certain recommendations for "Reading and Praying in the Vernacular." Despite the fact that they appeared nearly a decade ago, these practical, yet idealistic principles for "Reading the Word of God" still hold true today. They form, I think, a fitting conclusion to this chapter.

All Scripture readings are to be proclamations, not mere recitations. Lectors and priests should approach the public reading of the Bible with full awareness that it is their honored task to render the official proclamation of the revealed Word of God to his assembled holy people. The character of this reading is such that it must convey that special reverence which is due the Sacred Scriptures above all other words.

1. It is of fundamental importance that the reader communicate the fullest meaning of the passage. Without exaggerated emphasis or affectation, he must convey the particular significance of those words, phrases, clauses, or sentences which constitute the point being made. Careful phrasing and inflection are necessary to enable the listener to follow every thought and the relationship among them. Patterns of speech, especially monotonous patterns of speech, must be avoided, and the pattern of thought in the text must be adhered to. The message in all its meaning must be earnestly communicated.

36

2. The manner of speaking and tone of voice should be clear and firm, never indifferent or uncertain. The reader should not draw attention to himself either by being nervous and awkward or by being obviously conscious of a talent for dramatic reading. It is the message that should be remembered, not the one who reads it. The voice should be reverent without being unctuous, loud without shouting, authoritative without being offensive or overbearing. The pace must be geared to understanding—never hurried, never dragged.

3. By his voice, attitude, and physical bearing, the reader should convey the dignity and sacredness of the occasion. His role is that of a herald of the Word of God, his function to provide a meaningful encounter with that living Word. Perfection in this mission may not always be achieved, but it must always and seriously be sought.[25]

# Stories of Life and Faith

There is something at once unique and universal in our personal stories of life and faith. No one else ever has been, is or will be exactly like the individual I am. Yet there are elements in my life and faith story which transcend the particular details and apply to everyone.

These reflections of the lectors which follow fit into that category of the specific and, simultaneously, the general. Readers will, we hope, identify with certain aspects in each account and see them realized in their own lives and their experiences with this ministry.

The testimonies and people are true, but their names have been changed and their locations omitted.

*Chris is a highly placed executive in the health care field and the father of now grown and married children. A quiet, gentle and sensitive man, he still can be assertive and very efficiently gets jobs done. A dozen years ago he blazed the trail in his parish, serving as its first lector, leader of song and commentator for the revised Order of Mass. Today Chris coordinates the lector program. This story, however, relates his initial experience at the liturgy.

I remember the day that our pastor approached me and asked if I would read at the next Sunday's Masses.

This was to be a first for our parish, so I was apprehensive about the reaction of the parishioners and had doubts about my worthiness in assuming this responsibility.

Other parishes had already assigned laymen to lector roles and I had heard numerous negative comments about this innovation. These comments caused me to pause and reflect on what I was being invited to do.

I had read about the changes, and personally I was in agreement with them and the goals they were intended to achieve. After some reflection I realized that my participation would be a positive step toward the achievement of those goals.

As I rehearsed those first readings and studied the various parts of the Mass, anxiety increased and my self-confidence dwindled. In addition to the readings I was to lead the people in the hymns, even though our parish had never experienced congregational singing at Mass before this, and through the new format of the Mass using a missalette. I would not be able to use the St. Joseph Daily Missal which had been my "crutch" for years.

The Saturday before *that* Sunday was devoted almost entirely to preparation. I rehearsed the hymns with my daughter who would be playing the organ at Mass. I read the readings a "thousand" times.

What I knew about lectoring was very little, but I sensed that my role was to transmit to the congregation the basic messages which were contained in those written words and convey the mood and the thoughts which caused them to be written in the first place.

Sunday morning dawned and I prepared very carefully as I paced the living room floor, missalette in hand reading those words again out loud.

My wife and four daughters were as excited as I was and I recall their eyes reflected a slightly different light. I knew then that my life had changed.

Before I realized it I was standing behind the drape which led to the altar. Suddenly I pulled back the curtain and with heart pounding, roaring ears, and dry throat walked to the pulpit and announced the opening hymn.

I gazed upon the sea of faces which blurred before me and as I sang that hymn my tensions eased, the faces became individuals and I felt that I belonged.

The comments I received from parishioners as I left the church and the telephone calls afterward were most encouraging and gratifying.

Now a dozen years have passed since that day and hundreds of readings. I still find that my pulse quickens as I step forward to the pulpit to transmit the message contained in that Scripture.

*For some, to be a lector, particularly in the earlier days of the liturgical renewal, required overcoming obstacles and even opposition. Patricia experienced such roadblocks and hostility when she attempted to become, and later functioned as, her parish's first woman reader. This was a painful, trying time for her, especially in view of the fact that she had served for years as a true leader in the church and been close friends with some who vehemently opposed her efforts.

During the 1970's I started praying for God's complete guidance in my life.

Early in 1976 during my prayers, I felt God was calling me to lector at our church. I knew from past experiences that if my feelings were correct, God in his own way would let me know for sure.

I was concerned because there weren't any women lectors in the parish.

Later in the year I casually mentioned to two of my friends about lectoring and one said she too would be interested. I'm very thick-headed and I needed a strong confirmation that this was God's will and not just me and my imagination.

In September the confirmation came at a neighborhood party that my husband and I were at. The man in charge of coordinating the lectors' schedule was present, mentioned he was having a meeting for readers the following evening, and asked my husband if he would be interested in becoming one. My spouse said no, but I immediately spoke up and said I would. The coordinator seemed pleased that a woman was willing to lector and said he would inform the other men at that meeting. I judged that everything was settled and now I would be on the next lector's schedule.

However, one of my best friends, a reader at the parish, called our home the next afternoon and during the conversation I told him the coordinator was going to tell them I was being added as the newest lector. My friend said in no way was he going to let me, a woman, read in our church. He said he wouldn't let his mother and wife lector if they wanted to and, as my friend, he cared too much for me to let me read in church.

The director called me the following day and informed me that the request had not been supported by the reader's group. He suggested that I should go to our pastor. I didn't want to go alone. I called a girl friend who had told me earlier in the year that she wanted to lector and asked her to go with me.

The pastor said we could become lectors; that it was being done in some other parishes and he would handle everything.

Time passed and nothing happened. I was praying daily, and during my prayers thoughts started coming that maybe it wasn't God's will after all. I was becoming impatient. This impatient feeling was now in my prayers and thoughts.

One day during my prayers I felt that if it was God's will, it would come about on his timetable. I released the problem totally to God.

Later that week the pastor called me and told me he was going to put the announcement in Sunday's bulletin.

By now there were four women interested in lectoring and the pastor told me two other women had called him. We made arrangements to meet later that week.

When the day arrived for me to lector, I had practically memorized my reading. I was going to prove to our pastor and to my friend who had so strongly objected that women were as capable as men of serving God as lectors.

My reading was from the book of the prophet Isaiah (55:1–11). Unfortunately I demoted the prophet Isaiah to the private Isaiah.

On the outside I had confidence, but on the inside I was nervous. I wondered if my voice would be loud enough, if it would sound trembly. I had visions of shaky legs, of perspiring so much that I would float off the altar.

None of these things happened. Instead my nose started running. It still happens when I lector. God knows how to keep you humble.

Before Mass friends were wishing me the best and saying how happy they were for me; afterward many offered congratulations.

My objecting lector friend stopped talking to me, and that put quite a strain on our families since we had been best friends for over seventeen years.

I prayed to God about it. In my prayers I felt God said that I was not to worry, that I was not to serve man but to be open to serve him and that he wanted me regardless of what happens.

Once this victory for women occurred at our parish, a priest asked my daughter, a member of CYO, if she would represent the youth of the parish and become their first lector.

She did lector that year, and now whenever she is home from college and has the opportunity, she reads for our parish.

The night the coordinator of readers asked my husband if he wanted to lector and he said no, I guess it wasn't God's timing for him. After our daughter and I had been lectoring for a while, my husband then became a lector at the parish.

*For Betty, a single woman, career person and community organizer, the question of appropriate clothes is one of the factors she must be concerned about in preparing for her task. Here she discusses that situation and other steps of her regular routine prior to proclaiming God's Word at Mass.

First of all, I think it is important to state how special and privileged it makes one feel to be asked to be a lay lector.

Secondly, with the privilege goes a big responsibility. Maybe if I go through my routine I could explain that responsibility.

When I am scheduled to be a lay lector at Sunday Mass, I acquire a missalette (if I don't already have one for the month at home). I first read through the readings, then think about what the readings say. I normally read the passages over three or four times. This is to insure a clear understanding of all words, terms, and sentences. Biblical names at times can pose a problem, so I go over these enough to feel very comfortable pronouncing them without hesitation.

When I read at the Mass I am careful to speak loudly, clearly and with expression.

Usually I do not see the Prayers of the Faithful until I arrive at Mass. I like to read through these ahead of time to become familiar with them, especially the names for the sick and deceased petitions.

On the altar I consider myself as part of the whole and try to complement the entire Mass by singing the hymns along with the congregation, responding at various times through the Mass and assisting wherever necessary.

Perhaps this only affects women lay lectors, but appearance is also an important factor. I want to be sure my dress or suit is not flowery or flashy. I feel strongly about the fact that I want the congregation to hear what is being said and not being distracted by what the lay lector is wearing.

*Donald does a good bit of speaking before groups since he has been a teacher all his life and now functions as a high school principal. But nevertheless he felt awed, inadequate and nervous during his first appearance as a lector, even withdrawing from the position afterward for a few weeks to do some soul-searching. In his story Don describes these reactions and also mentions the impact this ministry as a reader has exerted upon his family.

I had always had a drive or some inner feelings of getting closer to God and the Church. I thought some of the ways to do this was to become involved as an usher, a Sunday collection counter, an officer in our Holy Name Society and to be very active in drives, social activities, and other church events: you name it and I was there taking part.

Although I did receive some satisfaction from these activities, none of those involvements satisfied that inner feeling of getting closer, as close as I possibly could, to

God. Even when praying privately, there was something lacking.

I was still searching and looking for that missing link between God and myself.

It was probably because of my involvement in these other activities that I was asked to be a lector.

I was happy and proud to be asked to lector. Because of my past experience as a teacher and high school principal I had no fears of going in front of a group of people and talking. I think the fears I did have were of inadequacy, the lack of knowledge or understanding of my religion and the lack of experience in proclaiming the Word of God. This to me was and still is an awesome responsibility. After all, in the past, this was a privilege reserved only for priests and religious. I remember the first time I lectored—I was as prepared to read as anyone ever was, and yet my knees were shaking, my palms had perspiration on them, and my voice was not mine, but some stranger's voice that I heard coming from within me.

In fact, because of those inadequacy feelings and the important role played by the lector, I stopped reading for several weeks and did some real soul-searching. After all, I felt that this was actually a ministry that God had chosen me for, and, like Thomas, I had my doubts.

But I still possessed that feeling and drive of getting closer to God, and lectoring was one of the avenues to accomplish this.

Serving as a lector has changed my life and the lives of my wife and four children. Sunday was always family day, beginning with Mass, but now Sunday is even more important and meaningful to us.

While preparing for the readings we discuss them as a family. After Mass, usually during Sunday dinner, we talk about them even more because we now have the opportunity to look at them again in the context of the liturgy. This ministry has brought me personally so much closer to God. While on the altar throughout the whole Mass, nothing exists in my awareness except God, the priest, and me. Subconsciously, I know my family is seated in "our" pew, participating in the Mass, but my whole being is involved in the Mass and the presence of Christ on the altar. It is a feeling of total satisfaction, a satisfaction I receive only when I lector.

*Although Wanda had graduated from a Catholic college and taught for several years before going to work in industry, her shy temperament and feelings of unworthiness made this thirty-year-old single woman reluctant to become a lector. She worked and prayed through that, however, and discovered that the ministry brought significant spiritual rewards with it.

My first experience reading before the congregation came during a family liturgy at which I read a short welcome before the Mass. I was very nervous and felt that a more outgoing person could have been much more effective. After Mass, the priest asked if I had ever considered becoming a lector. Being a lector was something that deep down inside I wished I was capable of doing, but I felt apprehensive of speaking in front of the congregation and unworthy to proclaim the Word of the Lord. From that time on though, I seriously started to consider the idea and prayed for guidance, but was unable to make any decision. My thought was that a lector should be someone who is a definite leader and not someone like myself, quiet and retiring. I now realize this concept was hindering me in making my decision—I was torn between what I really wanted to do for the Lord and what I felt I was capable of doing.

About five months after this first experience and while I was still praying for an answer, I passed a barber shop and noticed the priest there getting a haircut. As I waved, he motioned to me to come in. We exchanged greetings and he asked if I had signed up to become a lector yet. Naturally I hadn't, but that question in a barber shop was the answer that I had been waiting and praying for. It was all the encouragement that I needed and it helped me realize that I too could possibly serve the Lord as a lector because in my heart I really wanted to.

I've been a lector for five months now and enjoy it very much. When on the altar, I feel a special closeness to our Lord and my attention is more strongly focused on the Mass. I still have moments of nervousness, but in concentrating on my role as lector and in comtemplating the readings of the day, those moments seem to disappear. I feel I'm serving the Lord in a special way and feel honored to do so.

*Denise is a full-time housewife and mother who, however, has over the years found participation in the theater a useful hobby. Her natural talent and additional training as a thespian gave Denise good tools for the lector ministry, a function being carried on now by two sons, one at home and the other in college.

Being a parish lector has given me an opportunity to utilize one of my God given talents—the talent to be an effective reader with the ability to get across the Scripture message. I am not simply reciting something—I am helping the parish hear and reflect on the rich message of Sacred Scripture. I have had extensive training through the years as a performer in the theater—a thespian, you know—and that has helped nurture this native talent.

I desired to share my talent to help others and myself to hear the words of Christ. It has made by life richer and more meaningful. Many, many fellow parishioners stop me to say how well I read and that it is a joy to hear my voice interject meaning and feeling into the liturgy.

My children see the great joy I receive in lectoring and they likewise are proud to have me on the altar. They also see the time I spend in preparing the readings. They became inspired through this to want to lector. After permission was granted, I personally trained them. They were nervous in the beginning, but they soon found great joy in the readings and a greater meaning in their messages. Martin volunteered his services upon arrival at campus and is the head lector at his new parish, responsible for getting all the lectors assigned for the school year. Sean, my younger son, now lectors at our parish as well as heading the C.Y.O. We need to train our readers to be effective, not pick someone merely because they are [sic] a nice person. Delivering the Word should be treated as a ministry and a training process should be on-going.

On a few occasions, some of the readings left me very emotional. Raising adolescents is not an easy task in this present-day society and there have been at times many heartaches being a mother. But, somehow, it never failed that when I had to read after an especially hard interaction with my boys, it always seemed to be one that aided me as a parent to get across my message. There were a few occasions when tears came to my eyes and my heart became heavy with grief on the lectern; but God helped me through it, and my family, because I was the lector, got more meaning from the message. There were [sic] many a joyous family breakfast after Mass.

I am not "doing my thing," but am reading Scripture well enough so that my brothers and sisters are really listening. My personal satisfaction is immense—I am happy in my vocation and I put that across in the readings.

*Ralph had some questions seven years ago whether an Internal Revenue agent should function as a lector and eucharistic minister. He resolved that issue and, in his story, reflects on those years of service.

When the pastor first asked me to be a lay minister and lector, I was overcome by the honor of serving God and was apprehensive as to why I, a "publican" and "tax collector," would be given such an honor. I further wondered how the other parishioners would react to this wonderful honor bestowed on me.

I did not anticipate any problems with performing the required readings, since I am trained in public speaking. I was, however, very nervous about distributing the Eucharist. My early parochial school training by the sisters had taught me well regarding the proper devotion and respect being given to the Body of Christ. I found that to distribute his Body would cause my hands to actually shake, so badly at times that I could hardly hold the chalice. I have since rationalized these tasks, realizing that I am helping the priests and the parish members by my performance of those acts. I will to the day I die look upon this duty as the greatest honor I have ever received from my Church. I thank God every time I think of how lucky I am to be able to be so close to him.

I find that my experience over the past seven years and my familiarity with the rites have now made me become more assured of my role in the liturgy. I believe, however, that there should be certain requirements for any persons aspiring to become lectors or who are now lectors. Most importantly, all applicants would be screened to insure they are acceptable examples as Christians in the community. They should be able to present the readings and lessons with proper emphasis on spreading the Word of God. They should treat the honor of distributing the Body of Christ with grateful, reverential dignity. In addition, all lectors would be assigned temporarily for a one-year trial to evaluate their promptness, devotion to duty, diction and reverence. Continuation in this lay vocation would be dependent upon the lectors' abilities and the number of lectors available for the Mass schedules.

*Pamela teaches school and thus did not find the prospect of reading before others at all disturbing. But the awesomeness of proclaiming God's Word at holy Mass, the motives for wishing to do so and the ideal of truly interpreting the scriptural texts were strong challenges.

I have always liked going to Mass as long as I can remember. When the men began doing the readings, a new dimension was added to the Mass. I recall wishing that I could participate in that way. However, when the role of lector was offered to women, I hesitated. I really had to think through my motives: Did I think I was so great? Did I really have something to offer? Or was it vanity? Was I really trying to get closer to God through this effort?

After a couple of months of this confrontation, I became sure. The first time on the altar was awe-inspiring. I lost everything but my concentration on the sacrifice. I was indeed close.

Doing the readings was not too much of a challenge in itself as I perform this act many times in school. Trying to interpret, through my efforts, the words of Paul or the Old Testament was a far different goal, a goal that again seemed to bring me closer to God—as a lector but, more envelopingly so, at all the Masses I attend.

# The Word of God
# and the Book of Readings

### THE WORD OF GOD

While Moses was tending his father-in-law's flock he came to Horeb, the mountain of God, and discovered a bush which, though on fire, was not consumed. Curious about this phenomenon, he went over to examine it more closely. As he did so,

> God called out to him from the bush, "Moses! Moses!" He answered, "Here I am." God said, "Come no nearer! Remove the sandals from your feet, for the place where you stand is holy ground. I am the God of your father," he continued, "the God of Abraham, the God of Isaac, the God of Jacob." Moses hid his face, for he was afraid to look at God.[1]

That incident captures well the awesomeness, the transcendence of God. This being is totally beyond our comprehension, never fully to be understood, the Creator of heaven and earth before whom we remove our sandals, bow to the ground and hide our face.

By looking at the world around us we can reason to the existence of the Lord and even draw a few conclusions about God's nature. Birds singing at 6:30 in the morning, ocean waves ceaselessly pounding the shore, calm, clear, spring-fed lakes reflecting the beauty above and revealing rich life below, magnificent sunsets making viewers stand in wonder, sparkling stars and a full moon leading us to marvel and question how, how far, and why—these and other words of creation make it possible for humans to say: "Yes, there is a God who must be all-powerful, all-wise, perhaps all-good."

But just as in a sense we hide our face before the greatness of the Supreme Maker, so the face of God remains largely hidden from us. We may catch glimpses of the Lord through nature, but they remain just that—fleeting, uncertain glances.

However, this immense, incomprehensible God, in love and not out of any necessity, chose to draw back the veil which concealed those mysteries of the divine being. The Lord "many times and in various ways" has revealed—the word means remove or draw back the veil—the inner secrets of God's nature and how the infinite Creator wishes "to share with us divine benefits which entirely surpass the powers of the human mind to understand." Such self-disclosure we call divine revelation, and by it God has chosen to "manifest and communicate both himself and the eternal decrees of his will concerning the salvation of mankind."[2]

That divine revelation has been made or given to us basically in three ways: by the written Word of Scripture, the person of Jesus and the spoken Word of tradition.

Jesus Christ is the perfect revelation of the divine. He is the Word made flesh, the Son of God, while simultaneously the Son of Mary, the one who reveals the Father to us. God "sent his Son, the eternal Word who enlightens all men, to dwell among men and to tell them about the inner life of God."[3] Jesus told Philip, "Whoever has seen me has seen the Father."

Those divine realities, contained in the person of the God-made-man, likewise come to us through the inspired texts of the Bible, both the Old and the New Testaments, and through the equally inspired handing down by the spoken Word, preaching, example and institutions of our tradition.

The Vatican Council fathers summarized Catholic teaching on this important, but delicate matter of tradition, Scripture and the Church in these words:

> Sacred tradition and Sacred Scripture, then, are bound closely together, and communicate one with the other. For both of them, flowing out from the same divine wellspring, come together in some fashion to form one thing, and move toward the same goal. Sacred Scripture is the speech of God as it is put down in writing under the breath of the Holy Spirit. And tradition transmits in its entirety the Word of God which has been entrusted to the apostles by Christ the Lord and the Holy Spirit. It transmits it to the successors of the apostles so that, enlightened by the Spirit of truth, they may faithfully preserve, expound and spread it abroad by their preaching. Thus it comes about that the Church does not draw its certainty about all revealed truths from the holy Scriptures alone. Hence, both Scripture and tradition must be accepted and honored with equal feelings of devotion and reverence.
>
> Sacred tradition and Sacred Scripture make up a single sacred deposit of the Word of God, which is entrusted to the Church. By adhering to it the entire holy people, united to its pastors, remains always faithful to the teach-

ing of the apostles, to the brotherhood, to the breaking of bread and the prayers (cf. Acts 2:42). So, in maintaining, practicing and professing the faith that has been handed on there should be a remarkable harmony between the bishops and the faithful.

But the task of giving an authentic interpretation of the Word of God, whether in its written form or in the form of tradition, has been entrusted to the living teaching office of the Church alone. Its authority in this matter is exercised in the name of Jesus Christ. Yet this magisterium is not superior to the Word of God, but is its servant. It teaches only what has been handed on to it. At the divine command and with the help of the Holy Spirit, it listens to this devotedly, guards it with dedication and expounds it faithfully. All that it proposes for belief as being divinely revealed is drawn from this single deposit of faith.[5]

The Church believes that the Bible has been composed directly under God's inspiration, but with the Holy Spirit using human instruments to write down what words the Lord wished to have expressed. Once again, the bishops at the Council approved a statement which clearly and carefully explains the divine inspiration of Sacred Sripture.

The divinely revealed realities, which are contained and presented in the text of Sacred Scripture, have been written down under the inspiration of the Holy Spirit. For Holy Mother Church, relying on the faith of the apostolic age, accepts as sacred and canonical the books of the Old and the New Testaments, whole and entire, with all their parts, on the grounds that, written under the inspiration of the Holy Spirit (cf. Jn. 20:31; 2 Tim. 3:16; 2 Pet. 1:19–21; 3:15–16), they have God as their author, and have been handed on as such to the Church itself. To compose the sacred books, God chose certain men who, all the while he employed them in this task, made full use of their powers and faculties so that, though he acted in them and by them, it was as true authors that they consigned to writing whatever he wanted written, and no more.[6]

The Bible, then, is the work of God deserving our greatest respect and containing "firmly, faithfully and without error" all the truths the Lord wishes us to know for our salvation.[7] That fact or those beliefs serve as the basis for certain liturgical actions which dramatize the dignity of the Scriptures: printing the readings in a noble book, carrying the lectionary held high in procession, using candles at either side of the pulpit or lectern, incensing the volume at Gospel time, signing and kissing the text, developing a shrine for the Word in the church itself.

But the Bible is likewise the work of human authors who had different styles and approaches. Consequently, to understand what God wishes to communicate in a given passage or book, we must "carefully search out the meaning which the sacred writers really had in mind, that meaning which God had thought well to manifest through the medium of their words."[8]

Discovering that meaning requires a consideration of the literary form used, since the writers employed historical, prophetical, poetical and other diverse modes of literary expression. Moreover this search demands an examination of the situation and circumstances of a particular author's time and culture. In addition, it means that we must give regard "both to the customary and characteristic patterns of perception, speech and narrative which prevailed at the age of the sacred writer and to the conventions which the people of his time followed in their dealings with one another."[9]

The words of God, expressed in the words of human authors, are in every way like human language, just as the Word of the eternal Father, when in the person of Jesus Christ he took on himself the flesh of human weakness, because like us in all things except sin.[10] This human and divine element of the biblical text thus implies the need for that kind of prayerful reading, study and reflection recommended in an earlier chapter. It also explains why in the life of the Church the Scriptures have constantly been given such a hallowed place of importance, a point made well at the Second Vatican Council:

> The Church has always venerated the divine Scriptures as it venerated the body of the Lord, insofar as it never ceases, particularly in the sacred liturgy, to partake of the bread of life and to offer it to the faithful from the one table of the Word of God and the body of Christ. It has always regarded, and continues to regard, the Scriptures, taken together with sacred tradition, as the supreme rule of its faith. For, since they are inspired by God and committed to writing once and for all time, they present God's own Word in an unalterable form, and they make the voice of the Holy Spirit sound again and again in the words of the prophets and apostles. It follows that all the preaching of the Church, as indeed the entire Christian religion, should be nourished and ruled by Sacred Scripture. In the sacred books the Father who is in heaven comes lovingly to meet his children, and talks with them. And such is the force and power of the Word of God that it can serve the Church as its support and vigor, and the children of the Church as strength for their faith, food for the soul, and a pure and lasting font of spiritual life. Scripture verifies in the most perfect way the words: "The Word of God is living and active" (Heb. 4:12) and "is able to build you up and to

give you the inheritance among all those who are sanctified" (Acts 20:32; cf. 1 Th. 2:13).[11]

## THE BOOK OF READINGS

Those who have participated in pre-Vatican II Masses will remember well the familiarity of biblical readings both on Sundays and weekdays as well as at weddings or funerals. The same Sunday texts were repeated yearly; weekday liturgies had some variety, but often were Masses for the dead or repetitious common texts for a saint; weddings and funerals employed identical excerpts for every couple and each deceased person.

In reforming the liturgical books the Council fathers stressed as a key principle: "Sacred Scripture is of the greatest importance in the celebration of the liturgy. . . . Hence in order to achieve the restoration, progress, and adaptation of the sacred liturgy it is essential to promote that sweet and living love for Sacred Scripture to which the venerable tradition of Eastern and Western rites give testimony."[12]

Aware of the limited scriptural content in the liturgy we noted above, they made this general norm for revision more practical and specific by these directives:

• "In sacred celebrations a more ample, more varied, and more suitable reading from Sacred Scripture should be restored."

• "The sermon . . . should draw its content mainly from scriptural and liturgical sources. . . ."

• "Bible services should be encouraged, especially on the vigils of the more solemn feasts, on some weekdays of

Advent and Lent, and on Sundays and holydays, especially in places where no priest is available."[13]

• "Since the use of the vernacular, whether in the Mass, the administration of the sacraments, or in other parts of the liturgy, may frequently be of great advantage to the people, a wider use may be made of it, especially in readings, directives and in some prayers and chants."[14]

• "The treasures of the Bible are to be opened up more lavishly so that a richer fare may be provided for the faithful at the table of God's Word. In this way a more representative part of the Sacred Scriptures will be read to the people in the course of a prescribed number of years."[15]

Fulfillment of those directions by the Consilium for the Implementation of the Sacred Liturgy required the assistance of many scriptural and liturgical experts from all over the world. The task also took a long period of time. But the result, a book of readings or lectionary, has been one of the widely acclaimed, positive fruits of Vatican II.[16] That single volume lists texts for Sundays and feasts, for weekdays throughout the year, for Masses of the saints and for other special occasions.

The overall principles behind the arrangement of readings in this lectionary were these: to assign the texts of greatest importance to Sundays and feasts when the Christian people are bound to celebrate the Eucharist together and to locate other biblical readings which to some degree complement these Sunday or feast day passages in a separate series for weekdays.[17]

In this way the faithful would be able to hear the principal portions of God's revealed Word over a suitable period of time. However, neither the Sunday nor the weekday lectionary is dependent on the other.

*The Lectionary for Sundays and Feasts*

• The texts are arranged in a three-year cycle, designated by A, B, or C. How do you determine which cycle fits which calendar year? One starts with year C and works backward or forward. Year C is a year whose number is equally divisible by three, as if the cycle began with the first year of the Christian era. Thus, 1983 is cycle C; 1984, cycle A; 1982, cycle B, etc. There is a slight complication here: the cycles change or begin with Advent of the previous calendar year. Consequently, to illustrate, cycle B, which occurs in 1982, actually starts in Advent of 1981.

• Three readings are provided for each Mass: the first from the Old Testament (except during the Easter season when they are from Acts), the second from the writings of the apostles (from an epistle or the Book of Revelation, depending on the time of year), and the third from the Gospel. The conference of bishops in a country may permit only two readings, but the lectionary encourages use of all three, a procedure endorsed by our hierarchy in the United States.

This arrangement "illustrates the basic unity of both Testaments and of the history of salvation: a unity which has Christ in the memorial of his paschal mystery as its center, a unity which should be one of the main subjects of instruction."[18] Moreover, such an arrangement is traditional and has long been followed by the Eastern Churches.

• The readings are sometimes arranged according to a common theme or themes. The seasons of Advent, Lent and Easter best illustrate the thematic approach since each has its own spirit and message and all three biblical excerpts tend to reflect that or those particular theme(s).

• At other times, the readings are assigned according to a semi-continuous principle. The Sundays of the year thus have no particular or common theme. Their epistle and Gospel readings follow semi-continuously week after week, and the Old Testament passages were chosen because of their relationship to the Gospel.

• "The Old and New Testament readings best harmonize when their relationship is self-evident, that is, when the events and teachings of the New Testament are more or less explicitly related to those of the Old. The Old Testament readings in this lectionary have been chosen primarily because of their relationship to the New Testament selections, especially the Gospel reading."[19]

*The Lectionary for Weekdays*
• There are normally only two readings on weekdays.

• During the weekdays in the special seasons of Advent, Lent and Easter there is an annual arrangement of passages which reflect the themes of that time.

• On other weekdays, the Gospel selections are arranged also in an annual but semi-continuous series, so that Mark is read first (weeks 1–9), then Matthew (weeks 10–21), and finally Luke (weeks 22–34).

• During the thirty-four weeks "of the year" the first reading is arranged in a two-year cycle with separate, semi-continuous readings for alternate years. How do we determine which is year I, which year II? Series I is for the odd years, series II for the even years.[20]

*Lectionaries for Celebration of the Saints and Other Occasions*
• Some celebrations for saints have readings which are particularly pertinent to the individual saint and can be found in the Proper of the Saints—for example, the feast of St. Mary Magdalene on July 22.

• The Common of the Saints provides a more complete series of readings especially appropriate for different kinds of celebrations for the saints, texts generally applicable to many—for example, the feast of St. Dominic on August 6.

• The Lectionary for Ritual Masses, Masses for Various Occasions and Votive Masses provides a remarkably rich array of optional texts which enable the celebrant and the participants (couple for a wedding, parents for a baptism, bereaved family for a funeral, cluster of people for a special gathering) to select those which best fit the circumstances.

• A table in the back of the lectionary shows where a specific biblical text can be located in the lectionary itself. People who plan special small or large group liturgies find this helpful. After having picked passages from their Bibles, they then check the reference chart and find these excerpts in the lectionary for use at the actual celebration.

Prior to the Second Vatican Council, a single book contained all of the texts for Mass, including the readings. That was not the Church's practice from the start, a procedure which developed centuries ago as the priest assumed most of the roles in the liturgy.

The bishops at Rome have reversed this practice, clearly indicating that there are a diversity of tasks to be fulfilled by different individuals, including the priest. As a consequence we now have a lectionary or book of readings for the ambo, lectern or pulpit and a sacramentary or book of prayers for the altar and presiding chair. Essentially, the priest prays from the sacramentary while the reader and deacon (and occasionally the priest) proclaim from the lectionary.

Both of these volumes, however, should be substantial and beautiful publications or productions. The American bishops in their document on "Environment and Art in Catholic Worship" speak to that point:

> Any book which is used by an officiating minister in a liturgical celebration should be of a large (public, noble) size, with good paper, strong design, handsome typography and binding. The Book of the Gospels or lectionary, of course, is central and should be handled and carried in a special way. The other liturgical books of the Church, which contain the rites of our public worship tradition, are also worthy of venerable treatment and are a significant part of the liturgical environment. Each should be visually attractive and impressive. The use of pamphlets and leaflets detracts from the visual integrity of the total liturgical action. This applies not only to books used by ministers at the altar, chair and font, but also to those used in any other public or semi-public rite.[21]

This recommendation will make quite uncomfortable those lectors who customarily prepare from a missalette, pamphlet or printed sheet and prefer to read from such an item during the liturgy. The bishops' statement, nevertheless, rather clearly indicates that such a practice is inappropriate, since those materials do not suitably convey in symbol the dignity of God's Word.

Lectors in parishes which possess the Lectionary of Sunday Readings produced by the Pueblo Publishing Company should find the shift from missalette to lectionary not so difficult.[22] That volume—actually three volumes since there is a separate book for each of the A, B and C cycles—provides the scriptural passages "arranged in sense lines for easy reading" as the Roman directives suggest.[23] Moreover, since each volume contains only the one cycle of readings there is less possibility of confusion or mixup. In addition, the texts themselves have been produced in large, clear type with wide margins and helpful accents on difficult words.

Every Tuesday morning from 8:00–8:45 during the last two years of my pastorate at Holy Family Church in Fulton, New York, five Protestant ministers, an Episcopal priest and I gathered in the rectory to discuss the next week's homilies or sermons. That was possible because, among other reasons, the new Roman Lectionary had become the model for the reform of lectionaries in those other churches. All of us were using fundamentally the identical biblical reading for Sunday worship.

This practical consequence of liturgical renewal perhaps well exemplifes that the hopes of the Second Vatican Council and of Pope Paul VI in publishing a revised book of readings are being realized. Our late Holy Father expressed his aspirations in these words:

> The revision of the lectionary was indeed a wise directive, aimed at developing among the faithful an ever-increasing hunger for God's Word, the Word which leads the people of the new covenant to the perfect unity of the Church under the guidance of the Holy Spirit. We are fully confident that priests and faithful alike will prepare their hearts together more earnestly for the Lord's Supper, meditating more thoughtfully on Sacred Scrip-

ture, nourishing themselves daily with the words of the Lord. The fulfillment of the wishes of the Second Vatican Council will be the inevitable consequence of this experience of God's word: Sacred Scripture will become a perpetual source of spiritual life, an important instrument for transmitting Christian teachings, and the center of all theological formation.[24]

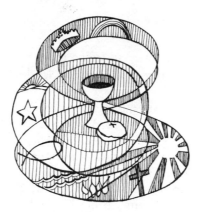

# The Church's Year of Grace

When Al and Sue Fiore sat around their dinner table reminiscing about grandparents, the wife remarked with pride that her grandfather, whom she had never seen, once was a policeman in London, the world's largest city.

Her husband looked at Sue and said, after ten years of marriage, "We should talk like this more often. I didn't know that about your grandfather. My own grandfather was a policeman also, in New York, the second largest city in the world."

There are two lessons to be learned from that incident. First, grandparents can be the family historians who give us roots, diminish the dangers of an unhealthy preoccupation with the present and link our past, present and futures together. Second, the family history normally, or at least frequently, comes to us through tales told around the table, much as Sue and Al discovered their common background over ice cream shared with a visitor in the dining room.

Our religious traditions and history likewise tend most often to be communicated in the context of meals, although ones which are special, sacred and ceremonial.

The Jewish Passover or seder meal well illustrates that point. At the beginning of this rite, a leader may say:

> Tonight we celebrate the Passover, the feast of freedom and redemption, and we read from the Haggadah. Haggadah is a Hebrew word meaning story. It is a special story. It relates our history: enslavement in Egypt, freedom, the holy commitment at Mount Sinai, and the return to the promised land. (The Haggadah ritual is called "seder," meaning "order" in Hebrew.[1])

In the course of the evening, a child asks four traditional questions—inquiries seeking answers why the various parts of the "seder" differ at a Passover celebration from the other more ordinary ritual meals.

> Why is this night different from all the other nights?
> On all other nights, we eat either leavened bread or *matzah;* on this night—only *matzah.*
> On all other nights, we eat all kinds of herbs; on this night, we especially eat bitter herbs.
> On all other nights, we do not dip herbs at all; on this night we dip them twice.
> On all other nights, we eat in an ordinary manner; tonight we dine with special ceremony.[2]

> The leader later responds:
> These are many questions. Now we begin to answer.
> Our history moves from slavery toward freedom.
> Our narration begins with degradation and rises to dignity.
> Our service opens with the rule of evil and advances toward the kingdom of God.[3]

Jewish children, then, learned about their roots or tradition in the context of this sacred banquet or meal. They heard annually the story of deliverance from bondage in

Egypt to the freedom of the promised land and that repetition kept alive these realizations to them.

When Jesus instituted the Eucharist he did so in the setting of such a Passover meal. At that time, Christ not only celebrated the seder ritual, but also gave us the sacrament of his body and blood and commanded his followers to celebrate Mass as a memorial, in memory of him. St. Paul described the eucharistic institution in this passage from his First Letter to the Corinthians, an excerpt used for the second reading on Holy Thursday's Evening Mass of the Last Supper:

> I received from the Lord what I handed on to you, namely, that the Lord Jesus on the night in which he was betrayed took bread, and after he had given thanks, broke it and said, "This is my body, which is for you. Do this in remembrance of me." In the same way, after the supper, he took the cup, saying, "This cup is the new covenant in my blood. Do this whenever you drink it, in remembrance of me." Every time, then, you eat this bread and drink this cup, you proclaim the death of the Lord until he comes![4]

Our Order of the Mass naturally carries out that injunction of the Lord Jesus to remember him, to do this in memory or remembrance of him and his living, loving deeds. In the third eucharistic prayer, for example, the priest prays immediately after the consecration or Lord's Supper section:

> Father, calling to mind
> the death your Son endured for our salvation,
> his glorious resurrection and ascension into heaven,
> and ready to greet him when he comes again,
> we offer you in thanksgiving this holy and living
> sacrifice.[5]

69

Celebrating day after day, week after week this holy, eucharistic, sacrificial meal does in fact keep alive and hand down our understanding and faith in the passion, death, resurrection and second coming of Christ.

Over the centuries, however, the Church has developed an additional way of preserving or handing down its central mysteries of belief. We term this the Church's year of grace. In that annual series, particularly the period from Christmas to Ascension, we see unfolded the complete cycle of Christ's mysteries, sometimes in abridged form, sometimes in their exact chronological order. Those mysteries of our Lord's life are thus lived over and over again, mainly in connection with a eucharistic celebration, but likewise through additional liturgical and paraliturgical services and elements.[6]

During the other seasons, Advent and Ordinary Time after Pentecost, we witness in a living, grace-filled way Christ's Spirit working in our midst through the Church, building up the kingdom of God and preparing for Jesus' coming in glory.

These annual celebrations, however, are more than mere historical recollections. They in fact contain unique graces within them for participants. True enough, such recurring feasts do fix in our minds those special events of salvation history and lead us to give praise and thanksgiving to the Father for them. Moreover, we can through such re-presentations contemplate the life of Jesus and through this reflection be led to imitate him. Nevertheless, it is the teaching of both great spiritual masters and the official Church that the Lord has attached certain proper graces to each of these mysteries and their celebrations.[7]

While it is the same Savior and the same work of salvation, each mystery of Christ contains a particular manifestation of the Lord, a special beauty, a unique splendor and a

proper grace. For example, the grace flowing from the celebration of Christmas differs from the grace emanating from
the celebration of Good Friday. We rejoice at the coming of
the Lord into our midst in one and experience regret for our
sins as we meditate upon the sufferings of Jesus in the other.[8]

The *Constitution on the Sacred Liturgy* of the Second Vatican Council succinctly summarized these notions on the
Church's year of grace in these brief paragraphs:

> Holy Mother Church believes that it is for her to cele-
> brate the saving work of her divine Spouse in a sacred
> commemoration on certain days throughout the course
> of the year. Once each week, on the day which she has
> called the Lord's day, she keeps the memory of the
> Lord's resurrection. She also celebrates it once every
> year, together with his blessed passion, at Easter, that
> most solemn of all feasts.

> In the course of the year, moreover, she unfolds the
> whole mystery of Christ from the incarnation and nativi-
> ty to the ascension, to Pentecost and the expectation of
> the blessed hope of the coming of the Lord.

> Thus recalling the mysteries of the redemption, she
> opens up to the faithful the riches of her Lord's powers
> and merits, so that these are in some way made present
> for all time; the faithful lay hold of them and are filled
> with saving grace.[9]

When Pope Paul VI authorized the revised general Roman calendar and liturgical year, he made his own the teachings of these spiritual writers and of the Second Vatican
Council. In particular, our Holy Father endorsed the notion
that these annual celebrations contain certain special graces
for those who participate in them.

These Popes, with the Fathers and the tradition of the Catholic Church, taught that the historical events by which Christ Jesus won our salvation through his death are not merely commemorated or recalled in the course of the liturgical year even though they instruct and nourish the least educated among the faithful. These Pontiffs taught rather that the celebration of the liturgical year exerts "a special sacramental power and influence which strengthens Christian life." We ourselves believe and profess this same truth.[10]

It would not be unreasonable to maintain that Roman Catholics have a grasp today of certain major mysteries of their faith more through this year after year repetition of feasts than through classroom instruction.

In addition, however, to this cycle of celebrations honoring the Lord—we call it the Proper Cycle—the Church year also recalls on several occasions the Blessed Virgin Mary, Mother of God, and officially recognized saints—we term that series the Sanctoral Cycle.

Through the latter she proposes such holy persons "to the faithful as examples who draw all men to the Father through Christ, and through their merits she begs for God's favors."[11]

Over the ages, the liturgical cycle nevertheless suffered certain unhealthy developments of false emphases. The Council fathers sought to correct those and gave some general principles for revision of the Church year. They are summarized below, and the pertinent reference from the conciliar text explaining each norm follows after the stated guideline.

• "Sunday as the Lord's Day and the weekly memorial of the resurrection should enjoy highest priority."

By a tradition handed down from the apostles, which took its origin from the very day of Christ's resurrection, the Church celebrates the paschal mystery every[1] seventh day, which day is appropriately called the Lord's day or Sunday. For on this day Christ's faithful are bound to come together into one place. They should listen to the Word of God and take part in the Eucharist, thus calling to mind the passion, resurrection, and glory of the Lord Jesus, and giving thanks to God who "has begotten them again, through the resurrection of Christ from the dead, unto a living hope" (1 Pet. 1:3). The Lord's day is the original feast day, and it should be proposed to the faithful and taught to them so that it may become in fact a day of joy and of freedom from work. Other celebrations, unless they be truly of the greatest importance, shall not have precedence over Sunday, which is the foundation and kernel of the whole liturgical year.[12]

• "The feasts of Christ the Lord should be given precedence over the feasts of saints or other celebrations."

The minds of the faithful should be directed primarily toward the feasts of the Lord whereby the mysteries of salvation are celebrated throughout the year. For this reason, the Proper of the Time shall be given due preference over the feasts of the saints so that the entire cycle of the mysteries of salvation may be suitably recalled.[13]

• "The Lenten season emphasizes two elements—baptism and penance."

The two elements which are especially characteristic of Lent—the recalling of baptism or the preparation for it, and penance—should be given greater emphasis in the liturgy and in liturgical catechesis. It is by means of them that the Church prepares the faithful for the celebration

73

of Easter, while they hear God's Word more frequently and devote more time to prayer.[14]

• "The feasts of saints (we celebrate them on their death date, or birthdate into heaven) should not take precedence over proper feasts, and only those saints of universal appeal should be in the general calendar. Others would be optional, local celebrations."

> The saints have been traditionally honored in the Church, and their authentic relics and images held in veneration. For the feasts of the saints proclaim the wonderful works of Christ in his servants and offer to the faithful fitting examples for their imitation.
>
> Lest the feasts of the saints take precedence over the feasts which commemorate the very mysteries of salvation, many of them should be left to be celebrated by a particular church, or nation, or family of religious. Only those should be extended to the universal Church which commemorate saints who are truly of universal importance.[15]

We will now go through the major seasons or feasts, point out their main theme or themes, and show how the lectionary or book of readings brings out the central aspect of those celebrations. Readers may wish to pass over this section and return to it later as a resource at the appropriate time, feast or season.

In any season, the most important day of the week is *Sunday.* According to the official *Roman Calendar:*

> The Church celebrates the paschal mystery on the first day of the week, known as the Lord's day or Sunday. This follows a tradition handed down from the apostles,

which took its origin from the day of Christ's resurrection. Thus Sunday should be considered "the original feast day."

Because of its special importance, the celebration of Sunday is replaced only by solemnities or feasts of the Lord. The Sundays of Advent, Lent, and the Easter season, however, take precedence over all solemnities and feasts of the Lord. Solemnities that occur on these Sundays are observed on the preceding Saturday.[16]

## ADVENT

The season of Advent has a twofold character. It is a time of preparation for Christmas when the first coming of God's Son to men is recalled. It is also a season when minds are directed by this memorial to Christ's second coming at the end of time. It is thus a season of joyful and spiritual expectation.[17]

On *Sundays,* each Gospel reading has a specific theme: the Lord's coming in glory at the end of time (first Sunday), John the Baptist (second and third Sundays), and the events which immediately prepared for the Lord's birth (fourth Sunday).

The Old Testament selections are prophecies mostly from Isaiah about the coming Messiah and messianic times.

The writings from the apostles are exhortations or instructions on different themes of the season.

On *weekdays,* the first series from Advent's beginning to December 16 contains a semi-continuous reading from Isaiah, including important passages also read on Sundays, with Gospel excerpts chosen because of their relationship to the Isaiah excerpt.

The second series from December 17 or the second

Thursday to December 24 centers on St. John the Baptist in the Gospel with the first passage either from Isaiah or from a text related to the Gospel.

The last week before Christmas has Gospels from the first chapters of Matthew and Luke which describe events immediately preparing for Christ's birth. Selections for the first reading are from different Old Testament books which include important messianic prophecies and a relationship to the Gospel.[18]

## CHRISTMAS

The Church considers the Christmas season, which celebrates the birth of our Lord and his early manifestations, second only to the annual celebration of the Easter mystery. The Christmas season runs from first vespers of Christmas until the Sunday after Epiphany, or after January 6, inclusive.[19]

### Sundays, Solemnities and Feasts

For the vigil and three Christmas Masses, the first reading is from Isaiah and the other passages, with two exceptions, follow the texts used in the pre-Vatican II Roman Missal.

On the feast of the Holy Family (Sunday within the Christmas octave), the Gospel tells of Jesus' childhood and the other readings touch on family life.

For the octave of Christmas and the solemnity of Mary the Mother of God, the Gospel and second reading are about the Virgin-Mother of God, and the Gospel and first reading speak of the naming of the child Jesus since this feast is no longer in the calendar.

The readings of the second Sunday after Christmas refer to the mystery of the incarnation; on Epiphany, the second reading speaks of the call of all people to salvation; the readings for the baptism of the Lord (Sunday after Epiphany) touch on that particular mystery.

*Weekdays*

The First Letter of John begins on his feast (December 27) and continues over the following days.

The Gospels present the Lord's manifestations, with Jesus' childhood from Luke (December 29–30), John's first chapter (December 31–January 5) and the significant manifestations recorded in the three Synoptic Gospels (January 7–12).[20]

### SEASON OF THE YEAR

Apart from the seasons of Easter, Lent, Christmas, and Advent which have their own characteristics, there are thirty-three or thirty-four weeks in the course of the year which celebrate no particular aspect of the mystery of Christ. Instead, especially on the last Sundays, the mystery of Christ in all its fullness is celebrated. This period is known as the season of the year.

The season of the year begins on Monday after the Sunday following January 6 and continues until Tuesday before Ash Wednesday inclusive. It begins again on Monday after Pentecost and ends before the first vespers of the first Sunday of Advent.[21]

The lectionary provides readings for all thirty-four weeks even though sometimes there are only thirty-three because certain seasonal feasts (e.g., Pentecost) and solemnities (e.g., Christ the King) replace these Sundays. They are so arranged, however, including the omission of a certain Sunday, that the eschatological readings with which the liturgical year concludes will still be read during the last two weeks of the year.

The Sunday celebrated as the feast of the Lord's baptism replaces the first Sunday of the year. Consequently, the weekday readings for the first week begin on Monday after the first Sunday following January 6.

The Sunday following the feast of the Lord's baptism is the second Sunday of the year, and the following Sundays are numbered consecutively until Lent begins.

The Sundays and weeks of the year after Pentecost begin according to a plan which is somewhat complicated. Referring to a church calendar or Order for Mass, both of which are normally available in the parish, to determine the appropriate week is probably the simplest and surest method of gaining that information. Once that is established following the feasts of Pentecost, Holy Trinity, and Corpus Christi, the Sundays proceed consecutively in a way that can be easily observed.[22]

*Sundays*

The *Gospel* for the second Sunday of the year refers to the manifestation of the Lord, already celebrated on Epiphany, with the traditional passage about the wedding at Cana and two other passages from John's Gospel.

The third Sunday of the year begins the semi-continuous reading of the three Synoptic Gospels with Matthew in year or cycle A, Mark in B and Luke in C. This thus provides a presentation of each Gospel's distinctive doctrine as well as a development of the Lord's life and preaching.

The above arrangement and distribution of texts also allows a certain harmony between the meaning of each Gospel and the development of the liturgical year. The readings after Epiphany are concerned with the beginning of the Lord's preaching and are related to his baptism and first manifestation, which are celebrated on Epiphany and following Sundays. At the end of the liturgical year the eschatological themes of these last Sundays occur in sequence because the chapters of the Synoptic Gospels which precede the passion narratives treat these themes more or less extensively.

In year B after the sixteenth Sunday of the year, there are five readings from the sixth chapter of John's Gospel (the teaching on the bread of life). This insertion is only natural since the multiplication of the bread in John's Gospel parallels the same narrative in Mark. In year C the first text in the semi-continuous reading of Luke (third Sunday of the year) is the preface to his Gospel in which he outlines his purpose for writing the Gospel; there did not seem to be another appropriate place for this reading.[23]

*Old Testament readings* were chosen for their relationships to each Gospel passage. This serves a twofold purpose: any great contrast between the readings in the same Mass is avoided, and at the same time the unity of Old and New Testaments is clearly shown. This relationship between the readings for each Mass is indicated by the careful selection of titles for the readings.

As far as possible the selection of readings has been made so that the texts are short and easy to grasp, but another purpose is to read the most important parts of the Old Testament on Sundays. Although these readings are ordinarily related to the Gospel passage and thus lack their own set order, nevertheless the treasures of the Word of God are opened up so that all who participate in Sunday Mass will hear most of the Old Testament's principal sections.[24]

79

Since the letters of John and Peter are read during the Christmas and Easter seasons respectively, the writings of Paul and James occur semi-continuously in the *second reading.*

Paul's First Letter to the Corinthians, lengthy and discussing so many different issues, has been divided over a three-year cycle at the beginning of this season of the year. Moreover, the Letter to the Hebrews has been broken into a section for year B and another for year C.

A table in the lectionary shows how these various books and readings have been arranged.

For the feast of *Christ the King,* the 34th and last Sunday, the theme of the readings centers on that mystery of the royal Jesus, "prefigured by David and proclaimed in the humiliations he suffered by dying for us on the cross, who governs and guides his Church until his return at the end of time."[25]

*Weekdays*

The *Gospel selections* are arranged so that Mark is read first (weeks 1–9), then Matthew (weeks 10–21), and finally Luke (weeks 22–34). The first twelve chapters of Mark are read in their entirety, omitting only those two passages from the sixth chapter which are read on weekdays at other times of the year. Everything omitted in Mark is read from Matthew and Luke. Thus all the elements which give the different Gospels their distinctive style and which are necessary for an intelligent understanding of each Gospel are read two or three times. The complete eschatological teaching of Luke's Gospel completes the readings of the liturgical year.[26]

Selections from either Testament, depending on the length of the book, occur in the *first reading.*

Extensive selections from the New Testament are included so that the listener is given something of each letter's

substance. Passages having little pastoral relevance today are
omitted.

The limited readings from the Old Testament are an attempt to give something of the individual character of
each book. The historical texts have been chosen for
their presentation of an overall view of the history of salvation before the incarnation. Lengthy narratives could
not be included; sometimes a few verses have been selected to make up a short reading. In addition the religious significance of some historical events is brought
out by selections from the wisdom books which serve as
introductions or conclusions to a series of historical
events.

Almost all the Old Testament books will be found in the
weekday lectionary in the proper of the season. The only
books omitted are the very short prophetic books (Oba-
diah, Zephaniah) and a poetic book not suited to reading
(Song of Songs). Some texts written for edification require a lengthy reading to be understood. Of these the
Books of Tobit and Ruth are read and the rest omitted
(Esther and Judith).

The Books of Daniel and Revelation are assigned to the
end of the liturgical year since they have appropriate eschatological themes.[27]

A table in the lectionary likewise outlines this two-year
arrangement of texts for the first reading.

## LENT

The season of Lent is a preparation for the celebration of
Easter. The liturgy prepares the catechumens for the cel-

ebration of the paschal mystery by the several stages of Christian initiation: it also prepares the faithful, who recall their baptism and do penance in preparation for Easter.

Lent lasts from Ash Wednesday to the Mass of the Lord's Supper exclusive."

The Alleluia is not used from the beginning of Lent until the Easter vigil.[28]

## Sundays

The *Gospel selections* for the first two Sundays recount the Lord's temptations and transfiguration as recorded in the Synoptic Gospels.

For year A the Gospel accounts concerning the Samaritan woman, the man born blind, and Lazarus are assigned to the following three Sundays. Since these passages are very important in relation to Christian initiation they may also be used for years B and C, especially when candidates for baptism are present. However, for pastoral reasons, many wished another choice of texts for years B and C and alternative selections have been provided: year B, John's text about Christ's future glorification through his cross and resurrection; year C, Luke's texts on conversion.

The *Old Testament readings* are about the history of salvation, one of the main topics of Lenten instruction. A series of texts has been prepared for each year to present the principal elements of this history from the beginning to the promise of the new covenant, especially readings about Abraham (second Sunday) and about the deliverance of God's people from slavery (third Sunday).

The selections from the *writings of the apostles* have been chosen because of their relationship to the Gospel and Old Testament readings, and as far as possible should harmonize with them.[29]

## Weekdays

The Gospel and Old Testament readings were chosen for their mutual relationship and for their treatment of various themes for Lenten instruction. Whenever possible, most of the readings from the Roman Missal were preserved. It seemed best, however, to arrange the readings from John's Gospel in a better sequence since most of it used to be read without any special order. Therefore a semi-continuous reading of John's Gospel, with a better relation to Lenten themes, begins on Monday of the fourth week.

Since the readings about the Samaritan woman, the man born blind, and Lazarus are assigned for Sundays only in year A (and are optional in years B and C), additional Masses with these texts have been inserted at the beginning of the third, fourth, and fifth weeks. During years B and C they may be used on any day of these weeks in place of the assigned weekday readings.[30]

## THE EASTER TRIDUUM

The Roman Calendar summarizes the purpose and main thrust of these three greatest days in the Church's year of grace.

Christ redeemed mankind and gave perfect glory to God principally through his paschal mystery: by dying he destroyed our death and by rising he restored our life. The Easter triduum of the passion and resurrection of Christ

83

is thus the culmination of the entire liturgical year. What Sunday is to the week, the solemnity of Easter is to the liturgical year.

The Easter triduum begins with the evening Mass of the Lord's Supper, reaches its high point in the Easter vigil, and closes with vespers on Easter Sunday.

On Good Friday and, if possible, also on Holy Saturday until the Easter vigil, the Easter fast is observed everywhere.

The celebration of the Lord's passion takes place on Friday during the afternoon hours.

The Easter vigil, in the night when Christ rose from the dead, is considered the "mother of all vigils." During it the Church keeps watch, awaiting the resurrection of Christ and celebrating it in the sacraments. The entire celebration of this vigil should take place at night, beginning after nightfall and ending before dawn.[31]

There is neither space nor hardly need to comment here on the rich array of biblical texts for these celebrations.

### EASTER

The fifty days between Easter Sunday and Pentecost are celebrated as one feast day, sometimes called "the great Sunday."

The singing of the Alleluia is a characteristic of these days.

The Sundays of this season are counted as the Sundays of

84

Easter. Following the Sunday of the Resurrection, they are called the Second, Third, Fourth, Fifth, Sixth, and Seventh Sundays of Easter or of the Easter Season. The period of fifty days ends on Pentecost Sunday.

The first eight days of the Easter season form the octave of Easter and are celebrated as solemnities of the Lord.

The Ascension is celebrated on the fortieth day after Easter.

The weekdays after the Ascension through Saturday before Pentecost inclusive are a preparation for the coming of the Holy Spirit.[32]

## Sundays

Until the third Sunday of Easter the *Gospel* selections recount the appearances of the risen Christ. To avoid interrupting the narrative, the reading about the Good Shepherd, previously assigned to the second Sunday after Easter, is now assigned to the fourth Sunday of Easter (that is, the third Sunday after Easter). The Gospels of the fifth, sixth, and seventh Sundays of Easter are excerpts from the teaching and prayer of Christ after the Last Supper.

The *first reading* is from the Acts of the Apostles, arranged in a three year cycle of parallel and progressive selections. Thus the life, growth, and witness of the early Church are presented every year.

The selections from the *writings of the apostles* are year A, First Letter of Peter; year B, First Letter of John; year C, the Book of Revelation. These texts seem most appropriate to the spirit of the Easter season, a spirit of joyful faith and confident hope.[33]

*Weekdays*

As on Sunday, the *first reading* is from the Acts of the Apostles, arranged semi-continuously.

The *Gospel readings* during Easter week tell of the Lord's appearances with the conclusions of the Synoptic Gospels reserved for the Ascension. A semi-continuous reading of John's Gospel follows, appropriate for the Easter theme and complementary to the Lenten readings. These readings are largely devoted to the teaching and prayer of the Lord after the Last Supper.[34]

# The Table of the Lord

Our Roman Catholic Mass has its roots in Jewish traditions and likewise parallels patterns in the public life of ancient Greece.

Rulers of Athens sent forth officially designated persons termed "heralds" who gathered together local inhabitants into a "duly summoned assembly." The Greek word for such a "duly summoned assembly" is *ekklesia,* from which comes the Latin noun *ecclesia* and eventually our English word "church."

These individuals, properly brought together according to the law, became a special body, a unique people ready to hear as a group the official message from their ruler. The herald then proclaimed his assigned text. Afterward the ek-, klesia or assembly pondered those words, weighed their impact, decided on suitable action in response and informed the messenger of their decision. He in turn carried that information back to the ruler.

In the Jewish traditions of the Hebrew Bible, individuals were similarly summoned to form the Qehal Yahweh or "the assembly of Yahweh." Thus molded into a unique gathering of people, they heard similarly from official messengers the words of their ruler and later pondered them and made an appropriate response. This reply was finally ratified or sealed by a deed—some ritual, sacrificial offering.

The ruler in their case, of course, was God. It was also God's Word which brought together the people, and it was to hear God's Word that they assembled.

In New Testament days, the apostles became the new heralds, with their task to call together the new elect of God, God's holy people, throughout the whole world. The Word of God, Jesus, sent them out, and it is the same word of Jesus now proclaimed to those people. That proclamation had a special name, "kerygma," and contained the fundamental message of Christianity. The holy people of God similarly reflected as a body on the message, then made their response as a group and sealed it with a sacrifice, the eucharistic meal.[1]

The liturgical scholar Louis Bouyer summarizes this overall structure of the Mass which reflects our secular and Hebrew background in these words:

> The liturgy in its unity and in its perfection is to be seen as the meeting of God's People called together in convocation by God's Word through the apostolic ministry, in order that the People, consciously united together, may hear God's Word itself in Christ, may adhere to that Word by means of the prayer and praise amid which the Word is proclaimed, and so seal by the Eucharistic sacrifice the Covenant which is accomplished by that same Word.[2]

Bouyer wrote that paragraph a decade before the Second Vatican Council. When the bishops and those who carried out their directives revised the Order of the Mass, however, they obviously preserved these concepts. The General Instruction of the Roman Missal thus delineates the general structure of a eucharistic celebration:

> The Lord's Supper or Mass gathers together the people
> of God, with a priest presiding in the person of Christ, to
> celebrate the memorial of the Lord or eucharistic sacrifice. For this reason the promise of Christ is particularly
> true of such a local congregation of the Church: "Where
> two or three are gathered in my name, there am I in
> their midst" (Matthew 18:20). In the celebration of
> Mass, which perpetuates the sacrifice of the cross, Christ
> is really present in the assembly itself, which is gathered
> in his name, in the person of the minister, in his word,
> and indeed substantially and unceasingly under the eucharistic species.[3]

Note the terms "gathers together," "the people of God," "priest presiding," "local congregation of the Church," and "assembly." The next article of that General Instruction further reflects those ancient movements of worship with its notions of the table of God's word and of God's body forming one act of worship.

> Although the Mass is made up of the liturgy of the word
> and the liturgy of the eucharist, the two parts are so
> closely connected as to form one act of worship. The table of God's word and of Christ's body is prepared and
> from it the faithful are instructed and nourished. In addition, the Mass has introductory and concluding rites.[4]

We see some practical consequences of this theory or analysis in the Church's insistence that only suitably prepared and designated persons serve as heralds, proclaiming God's Word.[5] Moreover, the inspired words of Scripture alone should be used, never replaced by secular texts regardless of how beautiful or seemingly appropriate.[6]

Finally, the actual ebb and flow of our Mass mirrors the pagan, Jewish and early Christian patterns. We gather as a body or people of God in the beginning and prepare to hear God's messengers and message. Heralds—lectors, deacons, priests—proclaim that to us in the two or three readings and the homily. We as an assembly duly summoned respond together to this proclaimed Word with the responsorial psalm, creed and general intercessions, ultimately sealing our response with the eucharistic sacrifice. These various elements and their relationships will be even clearer as we describe below in more detail the parts of the Mass.

There is an additional dimension to all of this, the element of faith. As the above quote stated, "Christ is really present" in the assembly, the minister, the Word, the eucharistic species. The proclamation of the Word not only makes the Lord present, but also stirs up our belief in Jesus' presence later in the liturgy of the Eucharist.

As a further point, we should mention that each of the renewed Roman rites observes this pattern, not simply the ritual for Mass. Thus, for celebration of the sacraments, blessings and burials the Church always recommends a liturgy of the Word and provides ample scriptural readings for these occasions.

We will now examine each part of the Mass, study its fundamental structure and make a few pragmatic suggestions or observations for the lector or reader.

### INTRODUCTORY RITES

The parts preceding the liturgy of the word, namely, the entrance song, greeting, penitential rite, Kyrie, Gloria, and opening prayer or collect, have the character of beginning, introduction, and preparation.

The purpose of these rites is to make the assembled peo-

ple a unified community and to prepare them properly
to listen to God's word and celebrate the eucharist.[7]

Forward-thinking parishes today often try to achieve the
purpose of these introductory rites by such creative and
sound steps as having greeters at the church entrances welcome people, offering a "good morning" or "good afternoon" from the altar, inviting on occasion persons to
introduce themselves to neighbors at the beginning of Mass,
starting the procession from the main vestibule and prolong-
ing the entrance song through sufficient verses and long
enough for the community to become stirred up and to sense
that members belong to one another.

Here are several practical points for the reader during
the introductory ritual:

• Ideally the commentator and lector(s) should be distinct and separate persons.

• The Church recommends that there be as many lectors as there are scriptural readings, e.g., on Sundays, the
priest celebrant or deacon and two readers.

• One of these lectors ought to carry in procession the
book of readings or lectionary. That volume, of substantial
size and noble beauty, should be held high, the base about
eye level, with its front facing forward. After a reverence to
the altar or tabernacle, the lector places the book on the altar
and goes to his or her seat in the sanctuary or among the congregation as local custom dictates.

• There are sound reasons for the lector(s) remaining in
the pews with the community during the introductory rites
and only coming forward when it is time to read.

• Normally and preferably, the community sings during the entrance procession and the reader naturally joins in that activity. The general instruction indicates what happens should there not be singing.

> If there is no singing at the entrance, the antiphon in the missal is recited either by the people, by some of them, or by a reader. Otherwise it is said by the priest after the greeting.[8]

Our American bishops, however, in their Foreword to the Roman Missal, indicate that the congregation should *not* join in this brief antiphon.

> Since these antiphons are too abrupt for communal recitation, it is preferable when there is no singing that the priest (or the deacon, other minister, or commentator) adapt the antiphon and incorporate it in the presentation of the Mass of the day. After the initial greeting, the priest, deacon or other minister may very briefly introduce the Mass of the day.[9]

The procedure by which a lector says: "Please join with me in reciting the entrance antiphon on page 1 of the missalette" has become so common that many priests and people, in my opinion, consider it required by liturgical law. As the bishops have noted, however, these sentences are so short that they make little sense by themselves and when recited by the entire congregation.

Their alternate recommendation is for the priest celebrant (or someone else like the commentator or lector), after his greeting, to introduce briefly the Mass, including the antiphon or an adapted form of it within his introduction. For example, on the Third Sunday of Advent, the priest celebrant (or someone else) after the greeting could say: "Today

we are at the mid-point of Advent and already begin to anticipate the joys of the Lord's coming at Christmas. St. Paul's
words set the tone for our celebration: 'Rejoice in the Lord
always; again I say, rejoice! The Lord is near.' Sin saddens
the heart. We now ask the saving God to forgive our sinfulness so we may truly celebrate this Eucharist with joy.''

## LITURGY OF THE WORD

Readings from scripture and the chants between the
readings form the main part of the liturgy of the word.
The homily, profession of faith, and general intercessions or prayer of the faithful develop and complete it.
In the readings, explained by the homily, God speaks to
his people of redemption and salvation and nourishes
their spirit; Christ is present among the faithful through
his word. Through the chants the people make God's
word their own and express their adherence to it
through the profession of faith. Finally, moved by this
word, they pray in the general intercessions for the
needs of the Church and for the world's salvation.[10]

The table of the Lord can be divided into two major
parts: the table of God's Word (the liturgy of the Word) and
the table of God's Body (the liturgy of the Eucharist). During the course of a Mass, these are three main focal points
within a sanctuary—the chair for the presiding priest, the
ambo or lectern for the readings and the altar for the eucharistic sacrifice. To underscore that distinction between the
two tables, some parishes have candles lighted beside the lectern for the liturgy of the Word which, after its completion,
are either extinguished or moved near the altar for the liturgy of the Eucharist. Others dramatize the Gospel's dignity
with a procession or have a large open Bible permanently located in front of the lector's stand.

Several pragmatic tips for the reader during the liturgy of the Word follow below:

• There are two or three scriptural readings depending upon the day or feast as noted earlier in this book.

• The titles are not to be read, although a brief introduction to each reading can be helpful.

• A dignified book should be employed for the proclamation, not a piece of paper or a pamphlet, again as has been suggested in a prior chapter.

• "Silence should be observed at designated times as part of the celebration. Its character will depend on the time it occurs in the particular celebration. . . . At the conclusion of a reading or homily, each one meditates briefly on what he has heard."[11] Such a silent pause after each of the biblical proclamations is perhaps the most frequently omitted element of the revised liturgy. In my experience, lectors tend to rush on, immediately announcing the page or the antiphon for the responsorial psalm, and organists or choirs instantly swing into the alleluia before the Gospel.

In my former parish, we instructed the readers to pray the Our Father to themselves and then to move on. That worked fairly well except in the case of one individual who misunderstood and instead said the Lord's prayer aloud.

• The responsorial psalm or gradual comes after the first reading. The psalm is an integral part of the liturgy of the word and is ordinarily taken from the lectionary, since these texts are directly related to and depend upon the respective readings. To make the people's response easier, however, some texts of psalms and responses have also been selected for the several seasons of the year or for the different groups of saints. These may be used, whenever the psalm is sung, instead of the text corresponding to the reading.

The cantor of the psalm sings the verse at the lectern or other suitable place, while the people remain seated and listen. Ordinarily the congregation takes part by singing the response, unless the psalm is sung straight through without response.

If sung, the following texts may be chosen: the psalm in the lectionary, the gradual in the Roman Gradual, or the responsorial or alleluia psalm in the Simple Gradual, as these books indicate.[12]

i. As the directives note, in effect any psalm may be used, not simply the one listed in the lectionary.

ii. Ideally, a cantor or the choir sings the verses and the congregation, supported by the cantor and choir, repeatedly chants the antiphon as needed.

iii. Songs or hymns should not replace a psalm at this point nor ordinarily should the psalm be omitted and an instrumental piece or extended period of silence substituted in its place. "The first reading is followed by a responsorial psalm, which is an integral part of the liturgy of the Word."[13]

iv. It would be best to have distinct persons exercise the roles of lector, cantor and commentator, although obviously a parish with limited personnel resources may find that impossible.

v. If the psalm is recited, the congregation may either join in the antiphon while the lector or commentator reads the verses or the community may recite the psalm in unison.

vi. As soon as feasible, lectors should omit unnecessary instructions like "Please join in the responsorial psalm on page 12." Such directives can be annoying, distracting, need-less and disrespectful of the congregation's intelligence. Except for special liturgies and unique arrangements, the people in the pews rather swiftly grasp the Mass's movement and the participation format.

> • According to the season, the second reading is fol-lowed by the alleluia or other chant.
> (a) The alleluia is sung outside Lent. It is begun by all present or by the choir or cantor; it may then be re-peated. The verses are taken from the lectionary or the Gradual.
> (b) The other chant consists of the verse before the gospel or another psalm or tract, as found in the lection-ary or the Gradual.
> When there is only one reading before the gospel:
> (a) during the time when the alleluia is sung, either the alleluia psalm, or the psalm and alleluia with its verse, or only the psalm or alleluia may be used;
> (b) during the time when the alleluia is not sung, either the psalm or the verse before the gospel may be used.[14]

i. "The alleluia or the verse before the gospel may be omitted if not sung."[15] Most liturgists recommend dropping the alleluia if it is not chanted. When, however, the alleluia will be recited, it would be desirable for the word to be re-peated three times each by the leader and congregation rath-er than the single repetition so common today.

ii. The lectionary provides the alleluia verse or the verse for the Gospel greeting during Lent. As with the psalms, however, there is great freedom to use whichever text best applies to the given Mass. The book of readings of-fers special texts for certain celebrations, but also seasonal or general ones which can be employed for a variety of other occasions.

iii. During Lent the alleluia is not sung with the verse before the Gospel. Instead one of the following (or similar) acclamations may be sung before and after the verse before the Gospel:

> Praise and honor to you, Lord Jesus Christ, King of
>  endless glory!
> Praise and honor to you, Lord Jesus Christ!
> Glory and praise to you, Lord Jesus Christ!
> Glory to you, Word of God, Lord Jesus Christ![16]

iv. The people stand for the singing of the alleluia before the Gospel.[17]

• In the general intercessions or prayers of the faithful, the people exercise their priestly function by interceding for all mankind. It is appropriate that this prayer be included in all Masses celebrated with a congregation, so that intercessions may be made for the Church, for civil authorities, for those oppressed by various needs, for all mankind, and for the salvation of the world.

As a rule the sequence of intentions is:

(a) for the needs of the Church,

(b) for public authorities and the salvation of the world,

(c) for those oppressed by any need,

(d) for the local community.

In particular celebrations, such as confirmations, marriages, funerals, etc., the list of intentions may be more closely concerned with the special occasion.[18]

i. The priest opens and concludes the general intercessions.

ii. The deacon, cantor or other person (usually, in practice, but not ideally, the lector) reads the petitions.

iii. The response should be varied occasionally, but not too frequently lest the community grow confused about the appropriate words to be said. Likewise, it is preferable to have a banner or some other display board with the response on it so the leader need not at each Mass say, "The response for today is. . . ." Finally, the response, which can be sung as well as recited, ought to be kept short and simple for easy congregational participation.

iv. When individual names for the sick and deceased are mentioned—a pastorally effective practice—the person reading the petitions should check these out carefully beforehand for correct pronunciation. It may even be wise for the priest celebrant, who normally knows the people better, to read them from a special card at the appropriate time.

v. The pause for special personal intentions ought to be prolonged sufficiently so that people can reflect and identify their individual needs. Too brief a hesitation ruins that petition's purpose and reduces it to a formalistic ritual.

## LITURGY OF THE EUCHARIST

At the Last Supper Christ instituted the paschal sacrifice and meal. In this meal the sacrifice of the cross is continually made present in the Church when the priest, representing Christ, carries out what the Lord did and handed over to his disciples to do in his memory.

Christ took bread and the cup, gave thanks, broke, and gave to his disciples, saying: "Take and eat, this is my body. Take and drink, this is the cup of my blood. Do this in memory of me." The Church has arranged the celebration of the eucharistic liturgy to correspond to these words and actions of Christ:

1. In the preparation of the gifts, bread, wine, and

water are brought to the altar, the same elements which Christ used.

2. The eucharistic prayer is the hymn of thanksgiving to God for the whole work of salvation; the offerings become the body and blood of Christ.

3. The breaking of the one bread is a sign of the unity of the faithful, and in Communion they receive the body and blood of Christ as the Apostles did from his hands.[19]

In Holy Sepulcher parish, Butler, Pennsylvania, a family prepares the altar after the liturgy of the Word has concluded. They bring forward an altar cloth, unfold it and arrange the necessary items for the liturgy of the Eucharist. Another family then brings to the sanctuary the bread, wine, water and offerings. Finally, the entire community unites enthusiastically with the eucharistic prayer, but in dialogue fashion, responding to the priest's proclamation through the appropriate words or song.

During this part of the Mass, the lector might keep these points in mind.

• It is highly desirable for the reader to use church envelopes and to drop them in the basket when passed, even if seated in the sanctuary and in clear view of all. That has a modeling, teaching value for others.

• The liturgical ideal, as mentioned, would have eucharistic ministers be distinct persons from lectors, but there is no Church prohibition against the same individual exercising a double role.

• The song during the communion of the priest and people expresses the spiritual union of the communicants who join their voices in a single song, shows the joy of all, and makes the communion procession an act of brotherhood. This song begins when the priest receives communion and continues as long as convenient. The communion song should be concluded in time if there is to be an additional hymn after communion.

An antiphon from the Roman Gradual, with or without the psalm, an antiphon with a psalm from the Simple Gradual, or another suitable song approved by the conference of bishops may be used. It is sung by the choir alone or by the choir or cantor with the people.[20]

• If there is no singing, the antiphon in the Missal is recited either by the people, by some of them, or by a reader. Otherwise the priest himself says it after he receives communion and before he gives communion to the congregation.[21]

The same recommendation of the American bishops noted in connection with the entrance antiphon applies here. The communion verse would best be said by an individual (commentator, lector, priest celebrant) rather than by the congregation. The priest could even work the verse or an adaptation of it into a brief invitation to come forward for communion. In any event, the very customary procedure, "Please turn to p. 15 and recite the communion antiphon," leaves much to be desired.

## CONCLUDING RITE

The concluding rite consists of:

(a) The priest's greeting and blessing which is on certain days and occasions expanded by the prayer over the people or other solemn form;

(b) the dismissal which sends each member of the

congregation to do good works, praising and blessing the Lord.[22]

A few observations for the reader at this part of the Mass:

• Announcements are made after the post-communion prayer and before the dismissal. They should be brief, with confidence that the congregation will read all the detailed comments in the bulletin handed to parishioners as they depart.

• It is neither necessary nor desirable always to have a hymn or community song at the recessional. Silence, a musical interlude or a choral piece can be a desirable alternative.

• One lector carries the book of God's Word out in the recessional just as it was borne into the church at the beginning, a noble book, held high, symbolizing the dignity of that text.

At the Lord's table each sign or sacramental action should be carried out with personal and prayerful faith, care, attention and enthusiasm by those who have special ministries to fulfill.[23] The lector is one of those unique ministers, and in the next chapter we will offer a number of positive and negative suggestions for the reader, recommendations which can help him or her discharge that function in an effective and suitable manner.

**8**

# Some Do's and Don'ts

In researching available material for this book in general and this chapter in particular I secured copies of several dozen publications which deal with the ministry of reading. Each one naturally takes its own approach, but most include sections offering some very specific directions on how to proclaim God's word properly. They treat of such important matters as posture, breathing, appearance, enunciation, preparation, training, nervousness and other equally significant issues.

The difficulty I encountered in studying these fine pamphlets or books produced by very competent religious leaders or speech experts was conflicting advice on certain identical points.

For example, all would agree that frequent eye contact with the community is an important, even essential ingredient of good public reading. However, how do you achieve this? Some urge looking directly at individuals; others warn readers *not* to gaze directly at individuals, lest a person in the pews grow uncomfortable or uneasy. Some recommend aiming at the back wall just over the heads of people in the final row (presuming there are no standers in the rear—a risky presumption in most Catholic churches); others stress the opposite and suggest looking at persons around the middle of the congregation.

Another illustration of contradictory directives from the experts centers on the best method for preparation. Several promote underlining in the text beforehand words which should be emphasized, going so far as to develop a system of colors, marks, and varied, multiple underscorings to indicate different levels of emphasis. Benedict Hardman, a man with excellent credentials—speech and English teacher, lector and commentator at a midwest college, former CBS network newscaster—explicitly, although in an afterthought kind of way, rejects that procedure and tells why:

> By the way, do not mark the material you are reading. If you do mark it, this will only result in mechanical, uninspired reading. If you are to make your reading an experience for yourself and for the congregation, it should be fresh and alive. You are reading the words of the great prophets and teachers. These words should be made as meaningful today as when first uttered.
>
> There is no set way to read any material. Reading, like speaking or singing, is an art. An art is not regimented. Art depends for its full force upon inspiration. If you mark your reading selection, you are in effect trying to follow footsteps in freshly fallen snow. You are trying to reconstruct slavishly a set pattern each time you read the selection. If you always read the same and do not take advantage of the heightened awareness you have when you are facing an audience, you will lose the vitality, the meaning, and the beauty of the passage. If you are concentrating fully on the reading material, your mind will guide your articulation processes. Meaning will dominate.[1]

The point about citing these two instances of conflicting recommendations is not to undermine the authors or their works, but to highlight the fact that good and competent persons disagree on the best ways of achieving noble goals. Moreover, each of the contradictory recommendations noted above has its own rationale and value. In fulfilling the ministry of lector therefore, as in nearly all matters of life, there are few, if any, absolute, uncontested, must-be-followed rules for preparation or execution. Every man or woman who assumes this awesome responsibility will need to fashion his or her own system, one which works most effectively and seems to produce the desired product—a vital, moving proclamation of God's inspired Word.

With that observation in mind, I now propose a rather overarching principle for readers and then ten "do's" and ten "don'ts." These come from my own quarter of a century experience as a parish priest and from the research of those texts, most of which will be found in the footnotes for this chapter.

### GENERAL PRINCIPLE: BE REVERENT, BE PREPARED, BE YOURSELF

"Be reverent" flows naturally and obviously from all that has been said in earlier chapters of this book. Aware of the dignity of the Bible's inspired character and of the reader's crucial function in worship, persons set aside for this ministry almost automatically will sense the attitude of reverence required before, during and after this task.

"Be prepared" hardly needs any explanation. However it is done and whatever steps are taken, careful preparation stands as one of those few absolute, uncontested, must-be-followed rules all guides and experts would support. If Frank

Sinatra rehearses so intensely for the cutting of a fragile disc, can we do less for the proclaiming of eternal words?

"Be yourself" keeps what follows below and has been written or said by others in perspective. All of us can improve, grow personally and become better at whatever tasks currently confront us. The lector is no exception. But reading God's message at liturgies has to be the Lord's work, not just ours. We are instruments only. That means preparing in the most effective way we can and praying for grace to do well, then simply being ourselves, albeit our best selves, before the people we serve.

## TEN DO'S

1. **Do be trained in advance.** Many dioceses and some parishes sponsor lector training workshops which run for a day, an evening or even several sessions. These normally include an explanation of the lector's role and extensive skill-building exercises to improve the reader's ability. Using audio recorders, video-tape equipment and skilled critics, such programs can prove extremely effective in enhancing the new or old lector's performance. For most effective results, however, these programs must involve small groups and they require considerable time to execute.

Participation in such a workshop would be ideal prior to beginning the actual exercise of the reader's ministry.

One can attempt to gain those skills and correct certain weaknesses privately and individually, but with greater difficulty and less success. Several manuals or books for readers go into some detail on these issues and provide exercises for personal remedial work. They cover, for example, breath control, projection, intonation, rate or tempo, phrasing, pauses, oral reading techniques, pronunciation, the microphone and other very specific matters. Five of the better publications are listed in the footnotes.[2]

**2. Do study the text beforehand.** At least some reading and study of the assigned passages at home prior to the liturgy enables the lector to proclaim with much better understanding and consequent feeling. It need not be as lengthy and in depth as a scholar might do, but here are a few simple steps which could be followed by the average parishioner.

(a) Obtain a copy of the full Bible, Old and New Testament, in the translation, probably either the New American or Jerusalem version, contained in the lectionary used at the parish. These, particularly the New American Bible, can be purchased at reasonable prices, but the lector should secure a text that includes the official footnotes.

(b) Early in the week, read over the text in the Bible itself, not from the missalette.

(c) Next read the whole chapter or the entire psalm from which the excerpt has been taken.

(d) Then study the introduction to the particular book and any footnotes given within the specific selection.

(e) Look up words whose meanings are unclear or pronunciations are uncertain. A list of commonly troublesome ones occurring in the lectionary can be found in Appendix I of this text. Telephone the parish or check before Mass with the clergy about proper names not found in the dictionary.

(f) Finally, if some commentary is available, research its observations on the passages assigned for the day's liturgy.[3]

**3. Do practice at home during the week.** After the study outlines above, begin preparation for the actual proclamation. Read over the texts silently once again. Then do so aloud. Finally, stand up and rehearse about five times, perhaps before a mirror or, better, in front of the entire family, inviting their comments.

Use of a tape recorder may be somewhat helpful, but that procedure contains the inherent danger of merely confirming the reader in certain bad habits of which he or she is not conscious. If we practice before others this risk is minimized. Moreover, if we can make our meaning clear in a rehearsal session before young children of the family, we should be able to accomplish the identical goal before an entire congregation.

4. **Do wear appropriate clothes.** While some parishes have introduced choir robes or albs for lectors, more generally and preferably, in my judgment, readers simply wear their "Sunday best" attire. We indeed should don our finest for the Lord, but, on the other hand, these clothes ought not to be distractions for the congregation. The people in the pews are to be drawn not to us, but to the Word spoken.

5. **Do know your church building.** This usually needs to be done only once, at the start of one's ministry, unless some exceptional complications arise like a malfunctioning public address system. A check on the size of the structure is important because a larger church requires longer pauses, more precise enunciation, a slower pace and greater attention to the vicissitudes of a microphone. The voice in these buildings must bear the brunt of the communication burden since facial expressions and even bodily gestures will be indiscernible for many in the congregation. A smaller church obviously offers a more inviting setting for oral interpretation, but here, too, each lector must evaluate the situation and judge what kind of volume, pause and pace will best serve his or her needs.

6. **Do arrive early.** Getting to the church on time for a

lector means about fifteen minutes early. This enables the reader to check the lectionary for the correct pages, to examine and rehearse the petitions for the general intercessions if this is the lector's responsibility, and to adjust the microphone's level and position. During that period, the reader could also go over the readings a final time, but on this occasion from the lectionary itself so that the physical layout of the words on the page is familiar. An early arrival also relieves anxiety for the celebrant and makes it possible for the liturgical ministers to spend some moments in silent and spoken prayer prior to the procession.

7. **Do process properly.** Ideally there should be as many lectors as there are readings, or two on Sundays. If the local policy, and a desirable approach at that, is for the readers to remain in their seats until needed, then one carries the lectionary in procession, while the other takes his or her seat with the community beforehand.

Walking in procession is not the same as a stroll or saunter in the park, nor is it a march. The ministers should move from one place to another gracefully and for a purpose, starting at a definite moment, following a determined route, traveling at deliberate speed and not looking around or gawking at people in the community.[4]

The lector should carry the lectionary and nothing else—no hymnal or missalette or pieces of paper. He or she holds the book, which should be large in size and noble in design, with both hands on the side or bottom, cross or design facing forward and opening to the left. The text should be held out about 18–24 inches before the face and elevated so that the bottom of the volume is at eye level.

On particularly solemn occasions, the book might be held at arm's length above the head with the cross facing back and visible to all the congregation.

When the procession reaches the sanctuary, after the customary reverence, the reader places the book either on the altar or at the lectern and takes his or her seat.[5]

In situations where the lectors remain with the congregation until time for the proclamation, they could follow this procedure nicely described by liturgist Father Eugene Walsh:

> At the time for the first reading, the people are sitting down after the prayer. The reader does not sit, but remains standing in place for a moment until there is quiet. This helps avoid the see-saw effect, the catapulting of reader into the reading space from the seated group.
>
> Let there be a moment's pause. We are beginning the first really important part of the celebration. Up to this point all has been preliminary. The reader moves directly to the lectern. She (he) moves with energy and dignity, not too fast, not too slow, and does not stop to bow or genuflect. The sign of the reader moving to place is itself an excellent sign announcing to the entire celebrating community that it is time to get ready. This sign helps to begin calling the people to attention.
>
> The reader takes time to open the book. The sign of opening the book is effective in its own right. It is a sign that says: We are about to begin. Be attentive.[6]

At the end, one lector should pick up the lectionary and recess out in similar fashion to the procession.

8. **Do begin firmly and pronounce proper words distinctly.** To begin firmly sets the scene, establishes a context and creates a climate. The lector should clearly indicate the book from which an excerpt has been taken and carefully pronounce proper nouns, including obscure Old Testament

names. The audience will very likely remember none of these seemingly inconsequential items. However, if the lector slides over or slurs them, a certain frustration unconsciously arises within the listener which ultimately will distract him. And once a hearer's attention slips, the reader must fight furiously to regain it.

9. Do maintain frequent eye contact with the listeners. Despite contradictory views on how a reader should best maintain eye contact with the congregation, experts unanimously maintain that this is not only a good, but an essential element of effective proclamation.

Moreover, whether one looks over the audience's heads or at a general area or directly into the eyes of a particular person, the reader needs to embrace during the course of a passage all parts of the church. Gazing now center, now left, now right, in a natural, easy, somewhat prolonged way will achieve this goal.

The eye contact, however, must be more than a furtive glance, a nervous, momentary bob of the head. That is and will appear artificial, a serious, compulsive movement, the response of a conscientious but unsure lector who has heard about the importance of eye contact and wants to fulfill that recommendation but fears losing his or her place in the text.

I have always found it helpful to use one finger on the page as a reference, permitting extended eye contact without fear of losing my spot in the passage. In the past year or so, with the usual mid-life deteriorating of vision, the value of such a practice has increased. One writer discourages the procedure and argues, "It should not be necessary to follow the text with the fingers. This is distracting for the listener. The best cure for this habit is constant practice in reading out loud."[7]

Our minor disagreement should not cloud concurrence

on the root issue—look as often as possible at the congregation, but without forgetting where you are in the text.

**10. Do use effective pauses frequently.** Remember that the pause is generally the reader's most powerful tool. It can convey a shift in the movement of a story and a change in the writer's thought pattern. It can mark off direct speech and heighten tension in preparation for an important sentence. It can give words an opportunity to reach people's ears and be absorbed by them. The pause, however, is a delicate instrument, albeit a potent one. It should be longer in a large building than in a small one, shorter for twenty-five persons than for twenty-five hundred. It should be frequent, but not too frequent; brief, but not too brief; extended, but not too extended.

The pauses after the reading and the words "This is the Word of the Lord" bear particular attention. Following "This is the Word of the Lord," readers should bow their heads and pause for a substantial period of reflection, and then return to their seats or move on to the next action.

### TEN DON'TS

**1. Don't fidget.** This is an understandable but distracting weakness among lectors. Being, standing and speaking in front of people will ordinarily be a challenging experience. Under such pressure we can, often unconsciously, develop fidgety habits with our head, arms, fingers, legs, feet or whole body.

Standing still in a relaxed, but attentive, commanding way with both hands resting lightly on the lectern helps to convey a sense of assurance. An openness to observations from family or friends of one's actual performance during a liturgy can provide a good test of whether the reader in fact

111

is still or fidgety and what mannerisms growing out of nervousness have crept into the lector's behavior.

2. **Don't start until the community is ready.** Before beginning the text, a lector should allow ample time for the audience to sit, cough, look around, squirm, turn pages and become comfortable. A silent pause until everyone appears ready to listen attracts attention and even gains the ear of those less disposed. Similarly, to pause for a few beats after the introduction to the readings aids in focusing a congregation's thoughts on the core of each passage.

Some churches follow the pattern of the symphony and theater, seating no one during the actual performance but waiting for a break in the action. Thus ushers hold back latecomers until the first reading has been completed, then seat people. They observe a similar approach throughout the second reading.

Protestant churches occasionally publish an order of service and hand these leaflets at the doors to members of the congregation as they enter. The text includes a phrase "Late arrivals will be seated at this point in the service."

Lectors do not have control over the distraction caused by the arrival and seating of late-comers, but at least they can be conscious of waiting for the maximum "settling down" of the congregation before proceeding with the proclamation.

3. **Don't keep others unduly waiting, but on the other hand don't move during common prayers.** This is a small but noteworthy point.

If the lector sits in the sanctuary, probably still the more usual procedure, he or she should *not* move to the lectern while the priest celebrant sings or recites the opening prayer. That distracts others and also conveys the impression that the lector does not really pray with others at Mass. Nevertheless, in the same arrangement, the reader should be ready to move as soon as the priest completes the prayer.

When the lector sits in the congregation and follows the system described above for that approach, this does not occur.

Similarly at the general intercessions, the lector who may read the petitions should wait until the creed has been finished before starting to the lectern. However, immediately, without hesitation the reader needs to move to the proper place and have the intercessions prepared for recitation. Otherwise there is an unnecessary break in the action, an interruption of the flow and a regrettable squandering of precious moments.

**4. Don't read from a missalette or typed sheet of paper.** Enough has been said in previous pages about why these alternatives are very undesirable. However, the frequency of their occurrence, the ease with which lectors slip into them and the sense of reassurance they give make it necessary to re-emphasize the desirability of proclaiming from a noble, dignified lectionary.

**5. Don't apologize for mistakes.** Benedict Hardman, the former broadcaster and speech teacher quoted earlier in this chapter, explains the reasoning behind this perhaps surprising recommendation:

> When you are set and begin reading, do not let an error in reading throw you. Even the best and most experienced broadcasters who constantly read orally encounter times when they make slips, or fluffs, as they call them. Some days these fluffs may be more frequent. They tend to occur when you do not concentrate on the reading material, or when you are tired or hurried.

As you become more experienced you will be able to take these mistakes in stride. Above all, you will learn not to go back to correct yourself if you think the meaning of the passage is clear. To go back to correct yourself only points up the error. Usually the congregation will not even notice if the content of what you are reading is fairly clear. We frequently make slips in our daily conversations and we do not even notice them. Nobody is completely fluent in speech, even when he is very sure of what he is talking about.

If you do fluff, forget it. It is the old idea of not crying over spilt milk. You will only compound your errors and lose your concentration on what you are reading if you worry about mistakes. You will destroy the continuity of the text you are reading if you continually correct mistakes. And above all, do not say "excuse me" if you make a slip. That expression completely destroys the meaning of what you are reading. It only draws attention to the reader and detracts from the reading. After all, you have not made a social error.[8]

6. **Don't mishandle or misuse a microphone.** That means, first, never cough or blow into the microphone. The first will magnify to enormous proportions your sneeze or cough throughout the entire church; the second, a mistaken way of testing a microphone, can actually injure the apparatus.

That means, second, don't strangle, clutch or hang on to the microphone. We are reading to the people, not to the microphone.

That means, third, don't rely too heavily or depend too much upon the microphone. The acoustics of a building ideally should be such that a microphone is not even required. However, in practice we must normally use one, but we should so project our voices that people may hear without aid of the microphone.

Some practice beforehand in the church itself with the microphone obviously is called for here. But since that type of rehearsal normally will be done in an empty church, some critique from listeners at a regular service would be desirable. Sound travels differently in a full and an empty structure.

7. **Don't read too rapidly or drop off at the end.** Nervousness can push us into speed-reading the text. We want to get it and the tension over with. Moreover, proclaiming at an ordinary, conversation pace will not do either. Large, reverberating churches require a much slower rate of reading. In addition, listeners cannot hear as well or absorb as fast in this context as they do in conversational exchanges.

We also have a natural tendency to lower our voice at the end of a sentence or to drop the final sounds of certain words. The public speaker or reader needs to be aware of this ordinary habit and take corresponding care to correct that trend.

8. **Don't read everything in the same way.** The lector may be reading introductions to the Scripture passages, the inspired text itself, the conclusion "This is the Word of the Lord," the petitions of the general intercessions and certain other comments. Moreover, the biblical excerpts will vary in style, including such diverse writings as poetry, prophecy, exhortation and history. These varied items should not be proclaimed in the identical manner, but each one ought to receive a slightly different method of proclamation.

The technical training I mentioned above would be extremely useful in developing these distinctive styles of reading.

9. **Don't hesitate to employ some breathing and relaxation exercises at home and just before the liturgy's start.** Once again Professor Hardman proposes some easy, practical and helpful steps in this regard:

> Relaxation is the key to unlock destructive nervousness. There are numerous exercises to aid relaxation. The basic one is deep breathing. Breathe deeply several times before you enter the sanctuary; you can take other inconspicuous deep breaths before you begin to read and while waiting for the congregation to settle down.
>
> Yawning helps relax the throat muscles and jaw. Actually, throat muscles should not be involved in speech. Their prime function is to aid swallowing. But if throat muscles are tight and tense, your voice pitch will rise and speaking will become an effort. The voice tires more easily. So yawn and softly say "ah-h-h" several times. Follow this with the vowels "a, e, i, o, and u" sounded in the same relaxed, easy manner.
>
> Another helpful exercise is to allow your head to sink to your chest. Slowly move your head from side to side while allowing your shoulders to droop at the same time. To get the full benefit of this exercise, allow your jaw to slacken and your tongue to hang. Obviously this is an exercise you will do in private!
>
> A simple exercise to learn proper control of breathing is to inhale fairly deeply. Check to see if your palm placed just below the rib cage moves outward. While exhaling slowly, count up to five. Gradually increase your count to ten as you do this exercise more often. You will not have to control your breath this long in normal speaking or reading, but this exercise gives you overall control. The amount of air you inhale is not as important as the control of air when you exhale.[9]

**10. Don't be afraid to be afraid.** The great opera star Lily Pons once admitted that she became "sick to her stomach" several hours before every concert performance. Noted Broadway actors have similarly acknowledged their nervous, frightened feelings before the curtain went up and discussed how they sought release in heightened conversation, physical exercise, silence and prayer.[10]

For a reader to experience parallel fears, nervousness, tension and anxiety prior to the liturgy is, consequently, a perfectly natural phenomenon and very likely a healthy, necessary one as well.

Those fears and tensions may manifest themselves in a variety of symptoms: a feverish feeling, rapid heartbeat, dizziness, difficulty in breathing, a dry mouth, sweaty palms and forehead, nausea, vomiting, diarrhea, knees knocking and general body tremors. Those anxieties may also overflow into other noticeable behavioral changes: staring, wandering eyes, weak trembling voice, vocalized pauses, tense or slovenly posture, leaning, swaying, rocking, and sometimes even laughing or crying.[11]

The lector, troubled by such inner and outer disturbances, can take comfort in the fact that the famous Roman orator Cicero experienced them. So did Abraham Lincoln and Winston Churchill.[12] One of the greatest of American actors, John Barrymore, also had trembling hands and butterflies in his stomach prior to an opening.

But Barrymore knew that this nerve-shattering ordeal nevertheless pulled the strings of his inner self tighter together and maintained his performance at a high pitch. He so recognized the value of such pre-performance agony that the actor actually became afraid if he was not afraid.[13]

How does a lector deal with those unpleasant, unsettling nervous fears?

First, by understanding that they are normal, natural

and in fact desirable. As in Barrymore's case, the tension sharpens our perceptions and enables us to proclaim the word more perfectly.

Second, by recognizing that the congregation for the most part is understanding and supportive. Few wish to exchange places with you. They tend to admire the "ordinary" lay person who has courage to stand before the congregation and do or say anything.

Third, by recognizing that a good portion of the congregation is quite apathetic and not overly interested in what the lector has to read, much less whether the reader is nervous or not.

Fourth, by facing the fear and acting against it, that is, by going ahead and reading at the liturgy. Ralph Waldo Emerson offered this advice about self-conquest: "Do the thing you fear to do and the death of fear is certain." George Bernard Shaw, when asked how he became an effective speaker, answered: "I did it the same way I learned to skate . . . by making a fool of myself until I got used to it."[14]

Fifth, by inviting someone to critique past performances, although not in a purely negative fashion. The positive feedback will help you realize how good has been the effort made.

Sixth, by experimenting with some of the relaxation and breathing exercises sketched in the preceding recommendation.

Seventh, by remembering that this is God's work, not ours alone. Jesus said, "Apart from me you can do nothing."[15] But St. Paul recalls words the Lord gave him when he begged three times for relief from an anxiety of his own: "My grace is enough for you, for in weakness power reaches perfection."

That great preacher, with his perspective now clarified, then went on to say, "And so I willingly boast of my weaknesses instead, that the power of Christ may rest upon me. Therefore I am content with weakness, with mistreatment, with distress, with persecutions and difficulties for the sake of Christ; for when I am powerless, it is then that I am strong."[16]

Lectors would do well do make those words of St. Paul their own.

9

# Cleanse My Heart and My Lips

Serving as a lector is a job, a function, a responsibility. But more than that, the person who reads in church fulfills a ministry, and a truly noble one at that, but only one of many flourishing in the Church today.

These various ministries cover five main activities—teaching, preaching, celebrating, organizing and individual pastoral care. Over the past few centuries those tasks seemed to have been reserved exclusively for ordained persons, bishops, priests and deacons, or consecrated religious, sisters and brothers under vows. However, in recent years, beginning around the 1960's, we have come to a different emphasis, recognizing that such functions or ministries are the privilege and responsibility of the total Church. Every member, through birth and baptism, is called by the Lord to exercise some ministry or ministries, the exact nature of which will depend upon the individual's particular gifts, the needs of the community to which he or she belongs, and the inner impulses of the Spirit.[1]

The reader fits precisely into that category. Through birth and upbringing, the lector has been gifted with certain natural abilities and continued training to read with understanding and speak publicly. Through Christian initiation—baptism, confirmation and the Eucharist—the reader has become a member of God's people, the body of Christ, a faith family. This body, made visible and specific in the local parish or worshiping community, has need of persons to study, pray over, prepare and proclaim the inspired biblical texts. Leadership people in that body articulate this requirement and extend invitations for volunteers to fulfill the demand. The potential lector becomes conscious of an interior inclination to respond affirmatively, accepting the general or individualized request for readers.

All of these ministries, of course, represent a sharing in the fundamental ministry of Jesus, his coming into the world to preach the good news and to save all by this paschal mystery of dying, rising and coming again. Every minister, including the reader, must then imitate not only what things our Lord did, but, perhaps more importantly, how he did them. A holy person, a man of prayer, a servant to others—Christ was each of those, and the lector, like all other ministers, should strive to follow in the Savior's footsteps.

"If a man wishes to come after me, he must deny his very self, take up his cross, and begin to follow in my footsteps."[2] "In a word, you must be made perfect as your heavenly Father is perfect."[3] "Be on guard, and pray that you may not undergo the test."[4] "But if I washed your feet—I who am Teacher and Lord—then you must wash each other's feet. What I just did was to give you an example: as I have done, so you must do."[5]

At the Second Vatican Council, the bishops issued a *Decree on the Ministry and Life of Priests.* In one paragraph they underscored the importance of holiness as an essential ingredient for the fruitful or successful fulfillment of a priest's ministry. I would like to take that statement and adapt it to lectors:

The very holiness of lectors is of the greatest benefit for the fruitful fulfillment of their ministry. While it is possible for God's grace to carry out the work of salvation through unworthy ministers, yet God ordinarily prefers to show his wonders through those men and women who are more submissive to the impulse and guidance of the Holy Spirit and who, because of their intimate union with Christ and their holiness of life, are able to say with St. Paul: "It is no longer I who live but Christ who lives in me" (Gal. 2:20).[6]

It follows that to fulfill properly the ministry of readers requires not only technical skills but inner holiness, not only proficiency in oral proclamation but preparation of a spiritual nature, not only study of the text but absorption of it into the heart, not only correct pronunciation of all words but loving imitation of the Word.

The preceding chapter centered generally on the first part of these requirements; this one has been designed to assist lectors with the second set of ingredients for a good reader.

### A PRAYER FOR READERS

The following prayer has been constructed from two sources: the Order of Mass and the ceremony for the Institution of Readers.[7] It could be recited privately at any time, of course, but the prayer might be particularly well suited as preparation just prior to reading the Bible, rehearsing the passages or studying the Scriptures.

> Almighty God, cleanse my heart and my lips
> that I may worthily proclaim your Gospel;
>
> bless my efforts to prepare,
> that I may meditate on your Word,

understand it better
and proclaim it faithfully to your people;

surround my ministry with your presence,
that I may carefully perform the task
entrusted to me,
preach Jesus Christ to others
announce the Word of God properly,
watch it grow in the hearts of listeners
and give glory to you, Father,
through your Son and in the Holy Spirit.

### BEFORE THE LITURGY

As we mentioned earlier, the lector should arrive about fifteen minutes before the start of a liturgy. In addition to the mechanical details which can be cared for in that time, it offers the reader a few moments to become recollected, to pray, and perhaps to join with the celebrant and other ministers for a period of silent or vocal prayer before the procession begins.

### PERIODS OF RENEWAL

From time to time we need to step aside and rest a while, to pull back and reflect on our lives, our work and our ministry. That may be accomplished through a day of retreat, an evening of renewal or a few extra moments of personal prayer and reflection. The series of reflective periods below might help in this renewal process.

Their pattern is a simple one: a patron saint to be invoked, a grace we seek, a scriptural passage, some reflection, a silent period of meditation, the concluding prayer for readers above. Obviously all types of variations and substitutions are permitted and encouraged.[8]

## 1. A Matter of Trust

*Patron Saint:* Abraham, our father in faith. Section II in the Book of Genesis, chapters 11–24, recounts the story of this great patriarch. Lectors would do well to read the entire account, although only one episode in that rich life of trust is noted below.

God, Yahweh, calls this obscure Semite out of a pagan land and summons him to travel from a comfortable nomadic existence in the desert to a strange territory and an unknown way of life. The Lord promises Abraham great blessings and the venerable patriarch simply believes in God's Word, proving that trust as he "went as the Lord directed him."

Later God promises to the old man, childless and without an heir, that he will have countless descendants. Once again, Abraham trusts blindly and "put his faith in the Lord, who credited it to him as an act of righteousness."

In Genesis 21 we note the fulfillment of that prediction in Sarah, Abraham's sterile, aged wife. "The Lord took note of Sarah as he had said he would; he did for her as he had promised. Sarah became pregnant and bore Abraham a son in his old age, at the set time that God had stated."

The Lord, however, submitted the patriarch to another test of his blind trust, faith and obedience. In a classic, touching story Abraham is fully prepared to follow God's strange request and sacrifice his beloved, wonderfully conceived son, Isaac.

*Grace Sought:* To trust with absolute, blind confidence in the midst of uncertainties and weaknesses that God will provide what may be lacking in my ministry as a reader.

*Scripture Reading:* Genesis 22:1–19.

*Reflection:* Abraham's response, "Ready," typifies the instant, great trust of the patriarch in God's goodness and fidelity. During the first eucharistic prayer we are reminded of this virtue when the priest celebrant mentions "Abraham, our father in faith." The application of his example to a lector's life should be evident.

*Silent Period of Meditation*
*Prayer for Lectors*

## 2. Fighting God's Will

*Patron Saint:* Moses and Jeremiah, the prophets

Most, if not all of us can easily recall or visualize the scene of a young child finding every kind of reason not to carry out a parent's request. Sometimes the excuses are simply ways of avoiding work, attempts that grow out of natural laziness or a reluctance to give up immediate pleasures (watching television, playing with friends, reading books). But at other moments the hesitation or resistance stems more from fear of the unknown or lack of self-confidence (a small child crying and clinging to the parent as dad or mom tries to teach the tiny tot how to swim).

Moses and Jeremiah mirrored some of that childish contrary behavior when God first called them to be prophets, to be mouthpieces of the Lord, persons who spoke for Yahweh.

Moses in particular repeatedly responded to God, "But, but, but . . . ," raising difficulty after difficulty, objection after objection why he could not or should not be the one to carry out the mission mentioned. The entire Book of Exodus would be a good project for a lector, but especially chapters 3–12. Listed below is an excerpt from that section which highlights Moses' recurrent reluctance and the Lord's ultimate anger at this rebellion.

Jeremiah's case, recounted more succinctly, is not so dramatic, but contains the same hesitation, a resistance based on the absence of self-confidence.

125

*Grace Sought:* To be prompt in carrying out God's will, "ready" as Abraham was, whenever the call to serve comes from an inner impulse or the voice of a parish leader.

*Scripture Reading:* Exodus 3:1—4:17; Jeremiah 1:4–10.

*Reflection:* Like the reluctant or resistant child, potential or veteran lectors may hesitate to respond when called because of diffidence or selfishness. The former can be overcome by an awareness that God will make up for our inadequacies; the latter may be conquered by the Lord's grace opening our hearts to a greater generosity in serving others.

*Silent Period of Meditation*
*Prayer for Lectors*

## 3. Cleanse My Heart and My Lips

*Patron Saint:* The prophet Isaiah appeared on the scene in Israel around the second half of the eighth century before Christ, at a time when the Jewish people were suffering blows from without and from within. Surrounding nations with their armies repeatedly threatened to crush God's chosen ones; many Israelites in the face of such dangers and out of weakness had undergone a moral collapse.

The account of Isaiah's call contrasts the majesty of Yahweh with the unworthiness of the future prophet and of the people to whom he belonged. God not only summons the prophet, but purifies his uncleanness.

*Grace Sought:* To recognize God's greatness and to seek the Lord's forgiveness which cleanses our sinfulness and makes us worthy to proclaim the sacred Word to others.

*Scripture Reading:* Isaiah 6.

*Reflection:* The scene for this chapter was the temple at Jerusalem, probably on some great feast, in the holy place before the holy of holies. Those six-winged creatures, partly human in form, were termed "seraphim" which means literally "the burning ones" and were often depicted in the art of the ancient Near East.

Out of reverence for the divine majesty they veiled their faces with two wings; out of modesty they concealed their extremities in similar fashion; out of readiness to do God's bidding, they extended their wings prepared for flight.

The triple "holy, holy, holy" expresses the superlative, the all-holy nature of God. That quality of holiness indicates the Lord's otherness, utter transcendence, complete apartness from anything sinful or merely finite. We recognize, of course, those words from the eucharistic liturgy, the Sanctus of the Mass immediately after the preface.

The smoke, a sign of the divine presence, recalls the clouds of glory which surrounded God and filled the tabernacle during the exodus and on Mount Sinai (see Exodus 19:16–19; 40:34; Deuteronomy 4:11). The noise and the shaking of the structure likewise are reminiscent of those events.

Isaiah felt doomed because popular belief held that anyone who saw God would die (see Genesis 32:31; Exodus 33:20; Judges 13:22).

The prophet, expressing his unworthiness before the majestic God, then experiences the Lord's initiative in cleansing Isaiah of sinfulness, an act symbolized by the burning coals or embers.

Just prior to the Gospel, the priest celebrant recites quietly a petition for cleansing of the heart and the lips based upon this incident in Isaiah's life, a formula which has been incorporated into the prayer for lectors.[9]

*Silent Period of Meditation*
*Prayer for Lectors*

## 4. Courage to Speak the Truth

*Patron Saint:* The prophet Ezekiel wrote in the sixth century B.C. This spokesperson for God addressed the chosen people during their exile in Babylon. He castigated the Israelites for their sinfulness, predicted the destruction of Jerusalem to the unbelieving Jews, and yet offered them hope for a restoration in the future.

Those were hard words to persons not always ready to hear such criticism. God, however, warned Ezekiel that this was to be his mission, urged him to have courage and reassured the prophet lest he grow fearful.

*Grace Sought:* To have courage when encountering criticism or opposition to my ministry as a messenger of God's Word.

*Scripture Reading:* Ezekiel 1:26—3:27.

*Reflection:* The lector probably will never face the kind of opposition Ezekiel did. He or she does proclaim God's word, a message which can convict people of their sinfulness and engender hostility. But normally this is not transferred to the reader. However, some in the community may resent the lector's role or criticize in unduly harsh terms the reader's performance. Such resentment and criticism wound, and it requires courage to learn from the negative remarks and to bear bravely the hurt feelings.[10]

*Silent Period of Meditation*
*Prayer for Lectors*


## 5. A Willingness to Listen

*Patron Saint:* Samuel. The initial three chapters of the First Book of Samuel contain the charming story of Samuel's beginning and early life. In reading through this account, the reader should note the parallels between these events and the situations involved in the birth of John the Baptist and Christ the Lord. For example, Mary's *Magnificat*, her song of praise after Elizabeth's greeting, reflects Hannah's prayer of thanksgiving.

*Grace Sought:* To listen with great openness to the Lord speaking through God's Word and other people.

*Scripture Reading:* 1 Samuel 3:1—4:1.

*Reflection:* In beginning a period of Scripture reading or study, we would do well to pick up the Bible, hold it reverently in our hands for a moment and reflect upon the truth that Christ is present in these pages. God will be speaking to me through these words. The example of Samuel, "Speak, Lord, for your servant is listening," becomes a model for us at such a moment.

*Silent Period of Meditation*
*Prayer for Lectors*

## 6. Christ Must Increase

*Patron Saint:* St. John the Baptist. We have mentioned earlier the value of reading all the Synoptic Gospel accounts of a particular incident and of checking the cross-references to other biblical texts as well as of examining the footnotes to particular sections.

To study the life of John the Baptist in detail as it occurs in the Gospels could, consequently, be a profitable venture from several points of view. First of all, it would provide the student with a total picture of this heroic figure. Secondly, it would exemplify how we can pick up additional insights and catch little nuances when we examine all the descriptions of an event.

To facilitate that process we have gathered here the scriptural references which mention St. John the Baptist and categorized them. The person without sufficient time to read through all of the texts may wish to move immediately to the single passage noted under "Scripture Reading."

*Conception and Birth*
Luke 1:5–25, 39–56, 57–80
(By studying all of chapters 1—2 in Luke's Gospel, the reader will note how the author has used parallel constructions to describe the conception, birth and early life of John the Baptist and Jesus)
*Preparing for the Lord*
Matthew 3:1–6; Mark 1:2–6; Luke 3:1–6; John 1:19–23
*Preaching Repentance*
Matthew 3:7–10; Luke 3:7–9
*Giving Some Guidance on Life's Obligations*
Luke 3:10–14
*Comparing Himself with the Messiah*
Matthew 3:11–12; Mark 1:7–8; Luke 3:15–18; John 1:24–28
*Baptizing Jesus*
Matthew 3:13–17; Mark 1:9–11; Luke 3:21–22; John 1:29–34
*Testifying about the Lord*
John 3:23–36
*Questioning Christ*
Matthew 11:2–6; Luke 7:18–23
*Being Praised by the Messiah*
Matthew 11:7–19; Luke 7:24–35
*Imprisonment and Death*
Matthew 14:3–12; Mark 6:17–29; Luke 3:19–20

*Grace Sought:* To let Christ and not myself shine through the reading of God's inspired Word.
*Scriptural Reading:* John 3:23–36.
*Reflection:* Purifying our motives is an on-going struggle

rather than a once and for all battle. We have been called to the ministry of reader not for our own gain and not to impress others, but to communicate the Lord's message to people of our worshiping community and to make Christ present for them through his Word. Like St. John the Baptist, we seek to make Jesus increase and ourselves decrease.

*Silent Period of Meditation*
*Prayer for Lectors*

## 7. Persons of Prayer

*Patron Saint:* Christ our brother. We preach Jesus as the Lord, but we also walk in the footsteps of him who is the way, the truth and the life. Christ was both Son of God and Son of Mary, divine, yet human. The Letter to the Hebrews tells us: "We do not have a high priest who is unable to sympathize with our weakness, but one who was tempted in every way that we are, yet never sinned."

This master and model for us prayed often. That same letter observed: "In the days when he was in the flesh, he offered prayers and supplications with loud cries and tears to God, who was able to save him from death, and he was heard because of his reverence."[12]

We noted in the last section how a reading of all the Gospel texts referring to St. John the Baptist gives a more complete picture of that great hero-prophet. In similar fashion, examining the Gospels to discover Jesus as a man of prayer becomes a rich, fascinating experience.

We list below a few of the texts in which Christ appears as a person praying, sometimes alone, sometimes with a group, sometimes spontaneously, sometimes according to formal Jewish worship patterns, sometimes silently, sometimes crying out, sometimes with a brief phrase, sometimes in a torrent of words.[13]

131

Again, the individual without time to peruse all these texts may wish to read only one or a few and then spend some moments in reflection. For that person, the references under "Scripture Reading" describe two events which reveal in a particularly graphic way the element of prayerfulness present in our Lord's life.

Luke 3:21–22; Luke 6:12; Matthew 14:19; Matthew 15:36; Mark 6:41; Mark 8:6–7; Luke 9:16; John 6:11; Luke 9:28–29; Mark 7:34; John 11:41–42; Luke 9:18; Luke 11:1; Matthew 11:25–27; Luke 10:21–22; Matthew 19:13; Luke 22:32; Mark 1:35; Mark 6:46; Luke 5:16; Matthew 4:1; Matthew 14:23; Mark 1:35; Mark 6:46; Luke 4:16; Matthew 21:12–13; Matthew 26:26–30; Luke 24:30–35; John 12:27–28; John 17:1–26; Matthew 26:36–46; Luke 23:34, 46; Matthew 27:46; Mark 15:34; Hebrews 7:25.

*Grace Sought:* To be a person of prayer, making time and space for it so that I may walk at every moment in the presence of God.

*Scriptural Reading:* Luke 1:12–16; Matthew 26:36–46.

*Reflection:* The life goal of a Christian is to walk continuously in the Lord's presence, thus praying constantly. But that ideal never can occur unless we regularly step aside, find time and space for quiet and enter into communion with the Lord. Despite the demands on Jesus from people who wished to hear his words and experience his healing touch, he, in the words of Luke, "often retired to deserted places and prayed" (Luke 5:16). Lectors, both as individuals and as a group, need such recurring periods of withdrawal for prayer if they hope to proclaim God's word from the heart.

*Silent Period of Meditation*
*Prayer for Lectors*

## 8. Hearing God's Word and Keeping It

*Patron Saint:* Mary, the mother of Christ. The greatness of our Lady is not only the fact that she was the Mother of Jesus and thus the Mother of God, a wonderful witness of divine power working in and through a human instrument. While that serves as the fundamental basis for honoring her, the Blessed Virgin also deserves our praise for the way she responded to God's many and diverse calls for service to others.

For example:

Once Mary understood what God wished of her at the annunciation, she replied "I am the servant of the Lord. Let it be done to me as you say" (Luke 1:26–38).

She immediately made a long journey to visit her elderly, pregnant cousin Elizabeth and assist the woman (Luke 1:39–56).

With Joseph she observed the Jewish tradition of presenting the Child in the temple (Luke 2:22–40).

After the anxious, confusing, unclear episode when her twelve-year-old Son was lost in the temple at Jerusalem, "his mother kept all these things in memory" (Luke 2:41–52).

When a couple faced embarrassment over the shortage of wine at their wedding in Cana, she interceded for them with her Son (John 2:1–12).

In the ultimate test of carrying out God's Word in practice, the mother on Calvary offered her Son and joined with him in the supreme work of saving us (John 19:25–27).

During those empty, expectant moments following the ascension of Jesus and before Pentecost she kept company with the still timid apostles and other close followers of her Son, supported them and united with these people as "together they devoted themselves to constant prayer" (Acts 1:12–14).

133

*Grace Sought:* To carry over into our everyday lives lessons from the Word of God we accept with our eyes and our ears through prayer, study and worship.

*Scripture Reading:* Luke 8:19–21; 11:27–28.

*Reflection:* In some ways it seems that Jesus here puts down his mother and minimizes her greatness, but not really. Christ instead emphasizes Mary's even more praiseworthy attribute of fidelity to God's Word. She is blest because she heard the word of the Lord and kept it.

*Silent Period of Reflection*

*Prayer for Lectors*

## 9. True to the Church

*Patron Saint:* St. Peter and St. Paul. The Church tends always to look at these men together, almost as twins, one who preached to the Jews, the other whose ministry centered on the Gentiles.

As visitors approach the front entrance of the huge and famous St. Peter's basilica in Rome, two statues on either side of the main piazza catch their attention: one is of Peter with the keys and the other of Paul with the sword, the one who as leader of the Church holds the keys to the kingdom of God and the other who, as tireless preacher throughout the world, proclaims God's Word which is sharper than any two-edged sword.[14]

The major celebration in the liturgical year of grace for these two pillars of our faith occurs on June 29. This solemnity of Sts. Peter and Paul, apostles, a holyday of obligation for the universal Church although not in the United States, as the title indicates honors both of them together.

The scriptural texts for the vigil and the solemnity itself contain the story of these men and their relationship to the

134

Church. The Gospels speak of Jesus' promise that Peter would be the rock foundation of his Church and his later bestowal of that position upon him (Matthew 16:13–19; John 21:15–19). The first two readings, from the Acts of the Apostles and the Letters of Paul, offer us a glimpse of Peter and Paul in terms of their fidelity to the message of Jesus, their position in the Church and their heroism in preaching the good news.

*Grace Sought:* To be loyal to Christ and the Church, that as the Church first received the faith from Peter and Paul, we may be kept true to their teaching.

*Scripture Reading:* Acts 3:1–10; 12:1–17; Galatians 1:11–20; 2:1–10; 2 Corinthians 11:16–33; 12:1–10; 2 Timothy 4:6–8, 15–18.

*Reflection:* As Roman Catholics we respect the position of the Pope, the Holy Father, as successor to Peter. Paul, despite his revelation from the Lord and mission to the world, recognized Peter's leadership as noted in the readings.

The lector serves as a minister of the Church, an official delegate of the bishop, a person specially designated to communicate a particular message. With that task goes a corresponding responsibility of being true and loyal to the Church, the bishop and the message served.

*Silent Period of Reflection*
*Prayer for Lectors*

## 10. A Warm and Living Love for the Bible

*Patron Saint:* St. Jerome. Born around 342, Jerome studied at Rome in his early years and acquired great skill and knowledge in Latin, Greek and the classical authors. Baptized there in 360, he began to follow a very ascetical life style, later traveled to the Near East and then became a hermit for four years during which he prayed, fasted, learned Hebrew and wrote a life of St. Paul. Afterward he was ordained to the priesthood and returned to Rome.

There Pope Damasus urged him to revise the Latin text of the Gospels, psalms and letters of St. Paul, a task which was to start in that holy city, and then be expanded and completed years later after he settled at a monastery in Bethlehem.

St. Jerome's greatest achievement was this enormous feat of biblical translation, translating into Latin the Old Testament from Hebrew and revising the extant Latin version of the New Testament. The Council of Trent, one thousand years afterward, designated his version, called the Vulgate edition, as the official Latin text of the Bible for Roman Catholics. Almost any Catholic translation from then until the mid-1900's was based on that Vulgate version which remained the authorized Latin text of the Scriptures until Pope John Paul II replaced it in 1979 with the New Vulgate.[15]

Jerome was a tempestuous person with a hot temper and caustic pen. But he had an equally intense desire for holiness and struggled mightily against his weaknesses. Throughout it all, however, was his great love for the Bible, which, augmented by his fine training and study, enabled him to provide the Church with so priceless a treasure of such lasting value.

Perhaps his most famous quotation, taken from a commentary he wrote on Isaiah, is: "Ignorance of Scripture is ignorance of Christ."[16]

*Grace Sought:* To foster that "sweet and living love for Sacred Scripture" which the Second Vatican Council urged for all followers of Christ.[17]

*Scriptural Reference:* Romans 15:1–6; 2 Timothy 3:10–17; Hebrews 4:12–13; 2 Peter 1:12–21; 3:14–18; Luke 24:13–35.

*Reflection:* Just as the lector as a person of prayer needs space and time for communion with the Lord, so the reader as a messenger of the Scriptures, a deliverer of God's Word to others, must find a daily period for prayerful study of the Bible.

*Silent Period of Reflection*
*Prayer for Lectors*

# Appendix I:
# Pronunciation Guide
# for Difficult Words

*These words occur in the first two readings and the psalm responses for the Sundays and feast days of the A, B and C cycles as found in the lectionary. A stressed syllable is indicated by CAPS.*

| | |
|---|---|
| Abel-meholah | AY-bel-mih-HO-lah |
| Abishai | ah-BEE-shy |
| Abraham | Ay-brah-ham |
| Abram | Ay-bram |
| Abyss | ah-BISS |
| Achaia | ah-KAY-ah |
| Acquittal | ah-QUIT-al |
| Admonish | ad-MAHN-ish |
| Ahaz | AY-haz |
| Alpha | AL-fa |
| Alpheus | al-FEE-us |
| Amalek | AM-eh-lek |
| Amaziah | AM-eh- ZIGH-ah |
| Ammonites | AM-en-ites |

| | |
|---|---|
| Amoz | AY-mahz |
| Antioch | AN-tee-ock |
| Anxiety | angz-EYE-eh-tee |
| Apollos | uh-PALL-oh |
| Apostle | uh-POSS-ul |
| Apostolic | AH-poss-TALL-ik |
| Aramean | ah-RAH-me-en |
| Arimathea | AH-ruh-muh-THEE-ah |
| Attalia | AT-uh-LYE-uh |
| Baal-shalishah | BAY-uhl-SHAL-ih-shah |
| Babel | BAY-bull |
| Barnabas | BAR-nah-bus |
| Barsabbas | BAR-suh-bus |
| Baruch | BAY-rook |
| Bethel | Beth-EL |
| Bethlehem | BETH-leh-hem |
| Bitumen | bih-TYOO-min |
| Brazier | BRAY-zee-er |
| Brigand | BRIG-end |
| Buffets | BUFF-ets |
| Caesarea | sez-uh-REE-uh |
| Caiaphas | KYE-ah-fas |
| Canaan | KAY-nan |
| Cappadocia | KAP-uh-DOH-she-uh |
| Carbuncles | KAR-bunk-els |
| Carmel | KAR-mel |
| Carnelians | kar-NEEL-yuns |
| Carousing | kah-ROUSE-ing |
| Cedar | SEE-der |
| Cephas | SEE-fus |
| Chaldeans | kal-DEE-ens |
| Cherubim | CHER-ruh-bim |
| Chloe | KLOH-ee |
| Chronicles | KRON-ih-kuls |
| Cilicia | se-LISH-uh |
| Circumsised | SIR-kum-sized |
| Cistern | SIS-tern |

| | |
|---|---|
| Colossians | Koh-LOSS-yuns |
| Consecrated | KON-seh-CRAY-ted |
| Corinth | KORE-inth |
| Corinthians | KORE-in-THEE-ens |
| Cornelius | KOR-neel-yus |
| Countenance | KOUNT-eh-nance |
| Covenant | CUV-eh-nant |
| Cretans | KREET-ens |
| Crucified | CREW-sih-fyed |
| Cyrene | SIGH-reen |
| Cyrenian | sigh-REEN-ee-an |
| Cyrus | SIGH-rus |
| Cushite | CUSH-ite |
| Damascus | duh-MASS-kus |
| Debauchery | de- BAWCH-er-ee |
| Decrepit | de-CREP-it |
| Derbe | DUR-bee |
| Descendants | de-SEND-ants |
| Deuteronomy | DEW-ter-RON-oh-mee |
| Diadem | DIE-ah-dem |
| Dissuade | dis-SWAYD |
| Dominations | DOM-in-NAY-shuns |
| Dromedaries | DRAHM-ah-dare-eez |
| Ebed-Mehlek | EH-bed-MEH-lek |
| Ecclesiastes | ek-LEE-zee-AS-teez |
| Edifice | ED-eh-fiss |
| Elamites | EH-lam-ites |
| Eldad | EL-dad |
| Eli | eh-LYE |
| Eliab | eh-LYE-ab |
| Eliakim | eh-LYE-eh-kim |
| Elijah | eh-LYE-jah |
| Elisha | eh-LYE-shah |
| Elite | ee-LEET |
| Ephah | EF-ah |
| Ephesians | ee-FEE-zyuns |
| Ephraim | EE-fraym |

| | |
|---|---|
| Ephrathah | EF-rah-thah |
| Equity | ECK-wit-tee |
| Euphrates | you-FRAY-teez |
| Ewes | USE |
| Exodus | EX-oh-dus |
| Expiated | EX-pee-ay-ted |
| Ezekiel | ee-ZEE-key-el |
| Ezra | EZ-rah |
| Famine | FAM-in |
| Fornicator | FOR-nih-KAY-tor |
| Galatia | guh-LAY-shah |
| Galatians | guh-LAY-shuns |
| Galileans | GAL-uh-LEE-ens |
| Galilee | GAL-uh-lee |
| Gehazi | geh-HAY-zee |
| Genesis | JEN-eh-sis |
| Gentiles | JEN-tiles |
| Gethsemani | geth-SEM-eh-nee |
| Gilgal | GIL-gahl |
| Gomorrah | go-MORE-ah |
| Habakkuk | HAB-eh-cook |
| Hadadrimmon | HAY-dad-RIM-en |
| Handiwork | HAND-ee-WORK |
| Hearth | HARTH |
| Hebrews | HEE-brooz |
| Hebron | HEE-brahn |
| Heifer | HEFF-er |
| Hilkiah | hil-KYE-ah |
| Hittite | HIT-ite |
| Holocausts | HALL-oh-costs |
| Horeb | HOH-reb |
| Hosea | HO-zay-ah or HO-zee-ah |
| Iconium | eye-KOH-nee-um |
| Illicit | ill-ISS-it |
| Immanuel | ih-MAN-you-el |
| Imperishable | im-PER-ish-ah-bul |
| Imputed | im-PEW-ted |

141

| | |
|---|---|
| Infidelity | in-FUH-del-ih-tee |
| Infirmity | in-FIR-muh-tee |
| Ingratiate | in-GRAY-she-ate |
| Iniquities | in-ICK-wuh-tees |
| Interrogation | in-TARE-roh-GAY-shun |
| Irreproachable | ir-re-PROACH-ah-bul |
| Irrevocable | ir-REV-ah-KAH-bul |
| Isaac | EYE-zak |
| Isaiah | eye-ZAY-ah |
| Israel | IZ-rye-el |
| Israelites | IZ-ray-el-ites |
| Jacob | JAY-kub |
| Javan | JAV-an |
| Jeremiah | JER-eh-my-ah |
| Jericho | JER-ih-koh |
| Jerusalem | jeh-ROO-suh-lem |
| Job | JOHB |
| Jonah | JOI I-nah |
| Joshua | JOSH-oo-ah |
| Josiah | JOH-sigh-ah |
| Judah | JOO-dah |
| Judaism | JOO-day-ism |
| Judea | joo-DEE-uh |
| Leprosy | LEP-roh-see |
| Levite | LEE-vite |
| Leviticus | leh-VIT-eh-kuss |
| Libel | LYE-bul |
| Libya | LIB-ee-ah |
| Luminaries | LOO-min-air-eez |
| Lyre | LYE-er |
| Lystra | LYE-struh |
| Maccabees | MAK-ah-beez |
| Macedonia | MASS-ih-DOH-nee-ah |
| Malachi | MAL-eh-kye |
| Malchiah | mal-KYE-ah |
| Malefactor | MAL-eh-FAC-tor |
| Malicious | mah-LISS-yus |

| | |
|---|---|
| Mamre | MAM-rih |
| Manifest | MAN-ih-fest |
| Manna | MAN-nah |
| Massah | MASS-ah |
| Matthias | muh-THY-us |
| Medad | ME-dad |
| Medes | MEEDZ |
| Megiddo | meh-GID-oh |
| Menstruous | MEN-stroo-us |
| Meribah | MER-ree-bah |
| Messiah | meh-SIGH-ah |
| Mesopotamia | MES-oh-poh-TAY-me-ah |
| Midian | MID-ee-en |
| Mitre | MY-ter |
| Moriah | moh-RYE-ah |
| Mosaic | moh-ZAY-ik |
| Mosoch | moh-SOCK |
| Naaman | NAY-uh-man |
| Naphtali/Naphthali | NAF-thuh-lee |
| Nathan | NAY-thun |
| Nazorean | NAZ-or-ee-an |
| Nehemiah | NEE-heh-MY-ah |
| Nicanor | NIK-an-oar |
| Nicolaus | NIK-oh-lus |
| Nineveh | NIN-uh-vuh |
| Oblation | oh-BLAY-shun |
| Offense | oh-FENCE |
| Olivet | OL-uh-vet |
| Omega | oh-MAYG-uh |
| Oracle | OAR-ah-kul |
| Oracular | oar-ACK-you-lahr |
| Ordinance | OAR-din-ance |
| Pamphylia | pahm-FILL-ee-uh |
| Paraclete | Pear-uh-kleet |
| Paralytics | PEAR-uh-lit-iks |
| Parmenas | PAHR-mee-nus |
| Parthians | PAHR-thee-ens |

| | |
|---|---|
| Paschal | PASS-kal |
| Patmos | PAT-moss |
| Patriarchs | PAY-tree-arks |
| Pentecost | PEN-tuh-cost |
| Perga | PUR-gah |
| Philippians | fuh-LIP-ee-ans |
| Phrygia | FRIDG-ee-uh |
| Pisidia | puh-SID-ee-uh |
| Plenteous | PLEN-tee-us |
| Pontus | PON-tus |
| Portico | POUR-tih-koh |
| Praetorium | pree-TOH-ree-um |
| Precept | PREE-sept |
| Prescription | pruh-SCRIP-shun |
| Primacy | PRY-mah-see |
| Principalities | PRIN-sih-PAL-uh-teez |
| Prochorus | PROCK-oh-rus |
| Profanation | PRO-fuh-NAY-shun |
| Prophecy | PROF-eh-see |
| Prophesy | PROF-eh-sigh |
| Pustule | PUS-tyul |
| Qoheleth | KOH-heh-leth |
| Recompense | RECK-um-penss |
| Reprobate | REP-roh-bait |
| Resplendent | ree-SPLEN-dent |
| Resurrection | RES-ur-RECK-shun |
| Revelation | REV-el-AY-shun |
| Revilement | ree-VILE-ment |
| Sabbath | SAB-bath |
| Salvation | sal-VAY-shun |
| Samaria | suh-MARE-ee-uh |
| Samuel | sam-YOU-el |
| Sanctified | SANK-tih-fyed |
| Sanctuary | SANK-tchoo-air-ee |
| Sanhedrin | SAN-heh-drin |
| Sapphires | SAFF-fires |
| Saul | SAWL |

| | |
|---|---|
| Scourge | SKURJ |
| Scythian | SITH-ee-un |
| Seraphim | SEHR-ah-fim |
| Shaphat | SHAY-fat |
| Sheba/Seba | SHEE-bah |
| Shebna | SHEB-na |
| Shechem | SHEE-kem |
| Shekel | SHEK-el |
| Shinar | SHY-nar |
| Shunem | SHOO-nem |
| Sieve | SEEV |
| Silas | SIGH-lus |
| Silvanus | sil-VAY-nus |
| Sinai | SIGH-nigh |
| Sirach | SEAR-rack |
| Sodom | SAH-dum |
| Sojourn | SOH-jern |
| Solicitude | soh-LISS-ih-tood |
| Solomon | SALL-oh-mun |
| Sosthenes | SOS-the-neez |
| Spiritual | SPEAR-it-YOU-al |
| Statute | STAT-yute |
| Steppe | STEP |
| Supplications | SUP-plih-KAY-shuns |
| Sympathizers | SIM-pah-THYZ-ers |
| Syria | SEER-ee-ah |
| Tarshish | TAR-shish |
| Tarsus | TAR-sus |
| Temerity | teh-MEHR-eh-tee |
| Terebrinth | TER-eh-brinth |
| Theophilus | thee-OF-uh-lus |
| Thessalonians | THESS-uh-LOH-nee-uns |
| Timbrel | TIM-brel |
| Timon | TIE-mun |
| Titus | TIE-tus |
| Transgressors | trans-GRESS-oars |
| Trepidation | TREP-uh-DAY-shun |

| | |
|---|---|
| Tribunal | try-BYOO-nal |
| Tubal | TOO-bul |
| Ur | OOR |
| Uriah | you-RYE-ah |
| Usury | YOU-sir-ee |
| Uzziah | you-ZYE-ah |
| Verdant | VER-dent |
| Vesture | VEST-yure |
| Vindication | VIN-dih-KAY-shun |
| Wadi | WAH-dee |
| Wrought | RAWT |
| Yahweh-yireh | YAH-way YIR-eh |
| Zarephath | ZAR-ih-fath |
| Zealot | ZELL-ut |
| Zebulun | ZEB-you-lun |
| Zechariah | ZEK-eh-RYE-ah |
| Zedekiah | ZED-eh-KYE-ah |
| Zephaniah | ZEF-eh-NYE-ah |
| Zion | ZIGH-un |
| Ziph | ZIFF |

# Appendix II:
# Rituals for the
# Commissioning or
# Institution of Readers

## *The Institution of Readers*

*Study Text 3*, published by the U. S. Bishops' Committee on the Liturgy includes two appendices on "The Institution of Readers" and "Ritual Mass for Ministers of the Church."

The former has been designed for a bishop or major superior formally instituting candidates in the ministry of reader. The latter has been published for more general use in celebrations involving a variety of ministers.

Pastors and parish worship committees who wish to have some kind of a commissioning service in their parishes for newly designated lectors may wish to take these rituals below and adapt them to their local situation.

### INTRODUCTION

1. Readers are instituted by the bishop or the major superi-

or of a clerical religious institute. The rite takes place during Mass or a celebration of the word of God.

2. The readings are taken in whole or in part from the liturgy of the day or from the texts suggested below.

## CALLING OF THE CANDIDATES

3. After the gospel, the bishop sits with his mitre on, and the appointed deacon or priest calls the candidates:

> Let those who are to be instituted in the ministry of readers come forward.

The candidates are called by name, and each one answers:

> **Present.**

They go to the bishop, before whom they make a reverence.

## INSTRUCTION

4. Then all sit and the bishop gives the homily, which he concludes by speaking to the candidates in these or similar words:

> God our Father revealed the mystery of salvation to us and brought it to completion through his Son made man, Jesus Christ. After proclaiming all that the Father had done, Christ entrusted his Church with the task of preaching the Gospel to every creature.

> As readers of the word of God, you are to help with this

task. You are accepting an important office within the people of God and are specially commissioned to serve the faith, which is grounded in the word of God.

It will be your responsibility to proclaim that word in the liturgical assembly, to instruct children and adults in the faith and prepare them for worthy reception of the sacrament, and to announce the Gospel, the good news of Christ, to those who do not already know it. Thus with your help men and women will come to know God our Father and his Son Jesus Christ, whom he sent, and so will be able to reach eternal life.

When you proclaim God's words to others, see that you are ready to accept it yourselves in obedience to the Holy Spirit. Meditate on God's word often, so that you will daily grow in God's love and by your way of life show forth to the world our Savior Jesus Christ.

### INVITATION TO PRAYER

5. Then all stand, and the bishop, without his mitre, invites the faithful to pray:

> Brothers and sisters,
> let us pray that God our Father
> will bless these his servants
> who are chosen for the ministry of readers,
> so that carefully performing the task entrusted to them
> they may preach Jesus Christ,
> and give glory to our Father in heaven.

All pray in silence for a brief period:

## PRAYER

6. Then the bishop continues:

God,
source of all goodness and light,
you sent your only Son, the Word of Life,
to make known the mystery of your love.
In your kindness bless + our brothers
who have been chosen for the ministry of readers.
As they meditate on your word,
help them to understand it better
and to proclaim it faithfully to your people.
We ask this through Christ our Lord.

R. Amen.


## INSTITUTION

7. Each candidate goes to the bishop, who gives him the Bible saying:

Receive this book of holy scripture
and announce the word of God faithfully
so that it may grow in the hearts of men.

The reader answers:
Amen.

Meanwhile, Psalm 19[18] or another appropriate song
may be sung, especially if there are many candidates.

8. If the institution of readers takes place during Mass, the
Mass continues as usual. If the institution takes place during

a celebration of the word, the bishop blesses the assembly and dismisses it in the usual manner.

## Ritual Mass for the Ministers of the Church

The new Roman Missal includes a ritual Mass for the ministers of the Church. The English translation proposed by the International Committee on English in the Liturgy is presented here for the purpose of study.

### 1. PRESIDENTIAL PRAYERS

All the presidential prayers, addressed to the Father, include the ministerial theme of the celebration. The opening oration draws inspiration from the text of Mark 10:43–45: ". . . anyone who wants to become great among you must be slave to all. For the Son of Man himself did not come to be served but to serve, and to give his life as a ransom for many" (see Mt 20:24–28; Lk 22:24–27). Another lesson in the leadership of service inspired the Prayer Over the Gifts: "If I, then, the Lord and Master, have washed your feet, you should wash each other's feet. I have given you an example so that you may copy what I have done to you" (John 13:14–15). The Prayer After Communion, adverting to the sacrament participated in, petitions for the grace that the ministers might be found faithful in their ministry of the gospel, sacrament, and charity: ("ut . . . fideles inveniantur Evangelii, sacramentorum caritatisque ministri") for the glory of God as well as the well being of the faithful whom they serve.

All three prayers follow the Roman or so-called classical structure: (1) the invocation to God the Father, (2) the petition on behalf of the faithful, and (3) the scope or reason for the request. The conclusions for the Prayer Over the Gifts and Prayer After Communion are the usual short form and clearly indicate the mediatorship of Christ emphasized since apostolic times. In the Letter to the Hebrews, for example, we read that "it is through him, then, that we must offer to God a continual sacrifice of praise, the tribute of lips that give thanks to his name" (Heb 13:15).

*OPENING PRAYER*

> Father,
> you have taught the ministers of your Church
> not to desire that they be served but to serve their
>     brothers and sisters.
> May they be effective in their work,
> and persevering in their prayer,
> performing their ministry with gentleness and concern
>     for others.
> We ask this through our Lord Jesus Christ, your Son,
> who lives and reigns with you and the Holy Spirit,
> one God, for ever and ever.

*PRAYER OVER THE GIFTS*

> Father,
> your Son washed the feet of his disciples
>     as an example for us.
> Accept our gifts and our worship;
> by offering ourselves as a spiritual sacrifice
> may we be filled with the spirit of humility and love.
> We ask this through Christ our Lord.

*PRAYER AFTER COMMUNION*

Lord,
you renew your servants with food and drink from
  heaven.
Keep them faithful as ministers of word and sacrament,
working for your glory
and for the salvation of those who believe in you.
Grant this in the name of Jesus the Lord.

## 2. SCRIPTURE READING

The following scriptural readings are suggested for the respective rites, whether celebrated within Mass or outside
Mass. For convenience, a reference to the *Lectionary for Mass*
is given in parentheses when applicable.

These scriptural texts offer those preparing for the liturgy a
wide range of options from which to select the most fitting in
view of the pastoral situation. Those to be instituted as readers or acolytes as well as those seeking candidacy to orders
should be encouraged to use the texts for the basis of personal prayer, reflection as well as group study and discussion
prior to the celebration or subsequent to it.

### FOR THE INSTITUTION OF READERS

Readings from the Old Testament

1. Deuteronomy 6:3–9 Keep these words in your heart.
   (no. 748)

2. Deuteronomy 30:10–14 Let the instruction of the Lord
   be near you. (no. 106)

3. Isaiah 55:10–11 The rain makes the earth fruitful.

4. Nehemiah 8:1–4a, 5–6, 8–10 They read from the book of Law and they understood what was read. (no. 458)

## Readings from the New Testament

5. 1 Corinthians 2:1–5 I have told you of the mystery of God.

6. 2 Timothy 3:14–17 All scripture is inspired by God and can profitably be used for teaching. (no. 357)

7. 2 Timothy 4:1–5 Preach the Good News; fulfill your ministry. (no. 358)

8. Hebrews 4:12–13 The word of God discerns the thoughts and intentions of the heart. (no. 144)

9. 1 John 1:1–4 What we have seen and heard we are making known to you. (no. 697)

## Responsorial Psalms

10. Psalm 18:8, 9, 10, 11.
    R. (cf. John 6:64b) Your words, Lord, are spirit and life.

11. Psalm 118:9, 10, 11, 12.
    R. (12b) Lord, teach me your decrees.

12. Psalm 147:15–16, 17–18, 19–20.
    R. (12) Praise the Lord, Jerusalem.

Alleluia Verse and Verse before the Gospel

13. John 6:64b and 69b Your words, Lord, are spirit and life: you have the words of eternal life.

14. Cf. Acts 16:14b Open our hearts, O Lord, to listen to the words of your Son.

15. The seed is the word of God, Christ is the sower; all who come to him will live for ever.

16. Cf. Luke 4:18 The Spirit of the Lord is upon me, he sent me to bring Good News to the poor.

## Gospel

17. Matthew 5:14–19 You are the light of the world. (no. 74)

18. Mark 1:35–39 He came preaching in their synagogues. (no. 75)

19. Luke 4:16–21 The Spirit of the Lord is upon me; he sent me to bring Good News to the poor. (no. 39)

20. Luke 24:44–48 Jesus sent the apostles to preach repentance for the forgiveness of sins. (no. 59)

21. John 7:14–18 My teaching is not mine, but of him who sent me.

155

# Notes

**CHAPTER 1**

1. Luke 4:14–22. Throughout this book, translations are from the New American Bible.
2. William Barclay, *The Daily Study Bible Series.* "The Gospel of Luke." Revised Edition. Philadelphia: The Westminster Press, 1975, pp. 44–47.
3. *Ibid.,* p. 48.
4. Joseph A. Jungmann, S.J., *The Mass of the Roman Rite.* Translated by Francis A. Brunner, C.SS.R., and revised by Charles K. Riepe. New York: Benziger Brothers, 1959, p. 259.
5. Barclay, *op. cit.,* pp. 46, 48.
6. Jungmann, *op. cit.,* pp. 1, 10.
7. Acts 2: 46.
8. Jungmann, *op. cit.,* p. 12.
9. *Ibid.,* p. 14.
10. *Ibid.,* p. 268.
11. *Ibid.*
12. *Study Text 3, Ministries in the Church.* Bishops' Committee on the Liturgy. Washington, D.C.: United States Catholic Conference, 1974, p. 24.
13. Jungmann, *op. cit.,* p. 268.

14. David N. Power, *Gifts That Differ: Lay Ministries Established and Unestablished.* New York: Pueblo Publishing Company, 1980, p. 73. I highly recommend this book for those who wish to study in more detail the complex and delicate history of lay ministries, including lectors, in the Church.

15. *Ibid.,* pp. 63, 70.

16. *Ibid.,* pp. 75–76.

17. *General Instruction of the Roman Missal.* Translated by the International Committee on English in the Liturgy, Inc. Toronto, Canada, 1969, article 66. The text appears in *The Liturgy Documents: A Parish Resource.* Chicago: Liturgy Training Program, 1980, p. 104.

18. *Study Text 3, op. cit.,* pp. 3–8.

19. Power, *op. cit.,* p. vii.

## CHAPTER 2

1. *Vatican Council II,* Austin Flannery, O.P., General Editor. Northport, New York: Costello Publishing Company, 1979. "Dogmatic Constitution on the Church," article 7, p. 355.

2. *Ibid.*

3. *Ibid.,* article 9, p. 359.

4. *Called and Gifted: The American Catholic Laity.* Reflections of the American Bishops Commemorating the Fifteenth Anniversary of the Issuance of the "Decree on the Apostolate of the Laity." National Conference of Catholic Bishops, November 13, 1980. Washington: USCC Publications Office, p. 4.

5. *Ibid.,* p. 5.

Just as by divine institution bishops, priests, and deacons have been given through ordination authority to exercise leadership as servants of God's people, so through baptism and confirmation lay men and women have been given rights and responsibilities to participate in the mission of the Church. In those areas of life in which they are uniquely present and within which they have special competency because of their particular talents, education and experience, they are an extension of the Church's redeeming presence in the world. Recognition of lay rights and responsibilities should not create a divisiveness between clergy and laity but should express the full range of the influence of the people of God. We see this and affirm it.

6. *Vatican Council II, op. cit.,* article 11, p. 361.

7. *Ibid.,* "Decree on the Apostolate of Lay People," article 10, p. 777.

8. *Growing Together: Conference on Shared Ministry.* Washington: USCC Publications Office, 1980, pp. 2–4.

9. *Vatican Council II, op. cit.,* "Dogmatic Constitution on the Church," article 12, p. 363.

10. *As One Who Serves,* "Reflections on the Pastoral Ministry of Priests in the United States." Prepared for the Bishops' Committee on Priestly Life and Ministry of the National Conference of Catholic Bishops. Washington: USCC Publications Office, 1977, p. 46.

11. *Growing Together, op. cit.,* pp. 16–17.

By baptism one enters into the dynamic of Jesus' life and death and into the demands of his mission. In this respect, all baptized are equally a part of the Church's mission. All baptized share in that priestly mission of Jesus and become a part of his fulfillment of his Father's will, of his bringing about of the kingdom here and now.

It also follows that if everyone becomes a part of that mission at baptism, everyone is also responsible for the fulfilling of that mission. Each person, according to the gifts and the talents received and according to the times and circumstances in which he or she lives, becomes responsible, with all others, for the fulfillment of the mission that Jesus gave to the Church. In this sense we talk quite rightly of shared responsibility. There is an old adage that when responsibility is shared with many, it becomes nobody's responsibility. The correct concept of Church, however, is that all are responsible but according to their own unique calling. In this sense unity is found in the shared responsibility, but the diversity and richness that come from various gifts are maintained and not reduced to the least common denominator. Ministry can only be discussed once that concept of Church has been assimilated.

Since all ministry has its source in Christ who gave to the

Church his own mission, ministry belongs to the whole Church; it is not something which belongs to the individual. It fosters and builds up the communion of all the faithful; it relates to the salvation of the world and the bringing of the good news to that world. Ministry, then, is something that is first in Christ and an essential part of his mission and then, by consequence, is in the Church which is his body. It has as its purpose building up that body of Christ with all its diversity and richness. It also relates to the Church's task of proclaiming the good news, the Gospel, to all, believers and unbelievers alike. It also is involved in that whole process of bringing divine life that comes with baptism in the Spirit to all people. In this sense it is closely involved in the call to holiness that all receive.

Ministry can be exercised only in the power of the Spirit. In order to maintain that beautiful and delicate balance between personal gift and the needs of the whole community, the presence of the Spirit that creates and builds unity is most important.

12. *Vatican Council II, op. cit.,* "Constitution on the Sacred Liturgy," article 14, pp. 7–8.

13. *Ibid.,* articles 28–29, p. 11.

14. *General Instruction of the Roman Missal, op. cit.,* article 58, p. 102.

15. *Ibid.,* article 34, pp. 95–96.

16. *Ibid.,* articles 66, 70, 71, pp. 104–105.

17. *Study Text 3, op. cit.,* p. 6.

CHAPTER 3

1. *Vatican Council II, op. cit.,* "Constitution on the Sacred Liturgy," article 7, pp. 4–5.

2. *Ibid.,* article 33, pp. 11–12.

3. *General Instruction of the Roman Missal, op. cit.,* article 8, p. 89.

4. *Ibid.,* article 9, p. 90.

5. *Ibid.,* article 33, p. 95.

6. *Ibid.,* article 34, p. 94.

7. *Ibid.,* article 35, p. 95.

8. *Vatican Council II, op. cit.*, "Constitution on the Sacred Liturgy," article 24, p. 10.

9. *Study Text 3, op. cit.*, p. 6.

10. *Vatican Council II, op. cit.*, "Dogmatic Constitution on Divine Revelation," article 25, p. 764.

11. *Study Text 3, op. cit.*, p. 52.

12. *Ibid.*

13. *Ibid.*, p. 6.

14. Geoffrey E. Wood, "Interiorizing the Lectionary." A chapter from *The Reader as Minister.* Edited by Horace T. Allen, Jr. Washington, D.C.: The Liturgical Conference, 1980, p. 53.

15. William Barclay, *op. cit.* A Protestant Scottish New Testament interpreter, the author has been well received by many Catholic scholars and students of the Bible, including the late Archbishop Fulton J. Sheen. He clashes in a few spots with Roman Catholic traditions, e.g., the virgin birth, but those are infrequent and the ordinary reader should be able to note or resolve these conflicts.

16. George Martin, *Reading Scripture as the Word of God.* South Bend, Indiana: Servant Books Distribution Center, 1975.

17. *Ibid.*, p. 7.

18. *Vatican Council II, op. cit.* "Decree on the Apostolate of Lay People," article 4, p. 770.

19. Gerard S. Sloyan, "Touchstones for Readers." A chapter from *The Reader as Minister.* Edited by Horace T. Allen, Jr. Washington, D.C.: The Liturgical Conference, 1980, pp. 81–84.

20. *Vatican Council II, op. cit.*, "Constitution on the Sacred Liturgy," article 29.

21. *Study Text 3, op. cit.*, p. 52.

22. *Norms on Eucharistic Practices.* Rome: Congregation for the Sacraments and Divine Worship, April 17, 1980. "Translation Issued by the Vatican." Paragraph 2.

23. John 15:5.

24. Philippians 4:13.

25. *Newsletter,* Bishops' Commission on the Liturgical Apostolate. December 1965.

**CHAPTER 5**

1. Exodus 3:1–6.
2. *Vatican Council II, op. cit.* "Dogmatic Constitution on Divine Revelation," articles 4, 6, pp. 751–752.
3. *Ibid.,* article 4, p. 751.
4. John 14:9.
5. *Vatican Council II, op. cit.,* "Dogmatic Constitution on Divine Revelation," articles 9–10, pp. 755–756.
6. *Ibid.,* article 11, pp. 756–757.
7. *Ibid.*
8. Ibid., article 12, p. 757.
9. *Ibid.*
10. *Ibid.,* article 13.
11. *Ibid.,* article 21.
12. *Vatican Council II, op. cit.,* "Constitution on the Sacred Liturgy," article 24, p. 10.
13. *Ibid.,* article 35, pp. 12–13.
14. *Ibid.,* article 36, p. 13.
15. *Ibid.,* article 51, p. 17.
16. *Lectionary for Mass.* Washington: United States Catholic Conference, 1969. The summary which follows in this and the next chapter has been taken from the introduction to the lectionary which appears in this paperback, a translation by the International Committee on English in the Liturgy.
17. *Ibid.,* article 2, p. i.
18. *Ibid.,* article 3, p. ii.
19. *Ibid.*
20. *Ibid.,* article 4, p. iii, article 17, p. xiv.
21. "Environment and Art in Catholic Worship," article 91. The text appears in *The Liturgy Documents: A Parish Resource, op. cit.,* pp. 239–240.
22. *Lectionary for Sunday Readings,* for A, B or C Cycle. Pueblo Publishing Company: New York.
23. *Lectionary for Mass, op. cit.,* article 24, p. xviii.
24. *Ibid.,* article 10, p. viii.

**CHAPTER 6**

1. *The Passover Celebration,* "A Haggadah for the Seder." Edited by Rabbi Leon Klenicki. Introduction by Gabe Huck. Produced by The Anti-Defamation League of B'nai B'rith and The Liturgy Training Program of the Archdiocese of Chicago. Chicago: Liturgy Training Program, 1980, p. 16.

2. *A Passover Haggadah.* The New Union Haggadah. Edited by Herbert Bronstein. New York: Grossman Publishers, 1974, p. 29.

3. *Ibid.,* p. 34.

4. 1 Corinthians 11:23–26.

5. *Order of Mass,* Eucharistic Prayer 3. Translation by the International Committee on English in the Liturgy.

6. Dom Columba Marmion, O.S.B., *Christ in His Mysteries.* St. Louis: B. Herder Co., 1939, p. 21. During my seminary training in the 1950's, this Benedictine scholar and writer was a frequently read and quoted expert in the spiritual life. That particular book developed in detail the notion of the Church year and the richness of its celebration. The following excerpt captures his teaching.

> Guided by the Holy Spirit, who is the Spirit of Jesus Himself, the Church unfolds before the eyes of her children, every year from Christmas to the Ascension, the complete cycle of Christ's mysteries, sometimes greatly abridged, sometimes in their exact chronological order, as during Holy Week and Paschal time. She thus makes each mystery of her Divine Bridegroom to be lived over again by an animated living representation; she makes us pass through each phase of His life. If we let ourselves be guided by her, we shall infallibly come to know the mysteries of Jesus and above all enter into the thoughts and feelings of His Divine Heart.

7. *Ibid.,* p. 25.

8. *Ibid.,* p. 22.

9. *Vatican Council II, op. cit.,* article 102, pp. 28–29.

10. *Roman Calendar.* Washington: USCC Catholic Conference, 1970, p. 4.

11. *Vatican Council II, op. cit.,* articles 103–104, p. 29.

12. *Ibid.,* article 106, pp. 29–30.
13. *Ibid.,* article 108, p. 30.
14. *Ibid.,* article 109, p. 30.
15. *Ibid.,* article 111, p. 31.
16. *Roman Calendar, op. cit.,* articles 4–5, pp. 7–8.
17. *Ibid.,* article 39, p. 12.
18. *Lectionary for Mass, op. cit.,* article 11, p. ix.
19. *Roman Calendar, op. cit.,* articles 32–33, pp. 11–12.
20. *Lectionary for Mass, op. cit.,* article 12, pp. ix–x.
21. *Roman Calendar, op. cit.,* articles 43–44, p. 13.
22. *Lectionary for Mass, op. cit.,* article 15, pp. xii–xiii.
23. *Ibid.,* article 16, p. xiii.
24. *Ibid.,* article 16, pp. xiii–xiv.
25. *Ibid.,* article 16, p. xiv.
26. *Ibid.,* article 17, p. xiv.
27. *Ibid.,* article 17, p. xv.
28. *Roman Calendar, op. cit.,* articles 27–28, p. 11.
29. *Lectionary for Mass, op. cit.,* article 13, pp. x–xi.
30. *Ibid.,* article 13, p. xi.
31. *Roman Calendar, op. cit.,* articles 18–21.
32. *Ibid.,* articles 22–26, pp. 10–11.
33. *Lectionary for Mass,* article 14, p. xi.
34. *Ibid.,* article 14, p. xii.

**CHAPTER 7**

1. Louis Bouyer, *Liturgical Piety.* Notre Dame, Indiana: University of Notre Dame Press, 1955, pp. 23–25.
2. *Ibid.,* p. 29.
3. *General Instruction of the Roman Missal, op. cit.,* article 7, p. 89.
4. *Ibid.,* article 8, p. 89.
5. *Norms on Eucharistic Practices.* Rome: Congregation for the Sacraments and Divine Worship, April 17, 1980. "Translation issued by the Vatican." articles 2, 3.
6. *Ibid.,* article 1.

7. *General Instruction of the Roman Missal, op. cit.,* article 24, p. 93.

8. *Ibid.,* article 26, p. 93.

9. *Ibid.,* "Foreword," section 18, p. 76.

10. *Ibid.,* article 33, p. 95.

11. *Ibid.,* article 23, pp. 92–93.

12. *Ibid.,* article 36, p. 96.

13. *Norms on Eucharistic Practices, op. cit.,* article 2.

14. *General Instruction of the Roman Missal, op. cit.,* articles 37–38, pp. 96–97.

15. *Ibid.,* article 39, p. 97.

16. *Ibid.,* section 36, p. 153.

17. *Ibid.,* article 21, p. 92.

18. *Ibid.,* articles 45–46, pp. 97–98.

19. *Ibid.,* article 48, p. 98.

20. *Ibid.,* article 56 i, pp. 101–102.

21. *Ibid.,* article 56 i, p. 102; section 19, p. 76.

22. *Ibid.,* article 57, p. 2.

23. *Music in Catholic Worship.* The text appears in *The Liturgy Documents, op. cit.,* paragraph 9, p. 192.


**CHAPTER 8**

1. Benedict Hardman, *Speech and Oral Reading Techniques for Mass Lectors and Commentators.* Collegeville, Minnesota: The Liturgical Press, 1966, pp. 17–18.

2. *Ibid.* Also cf. Raymond Clarke, *Sounds Effective.* London: Geoffrey Chapman, 1969; Charlotte Lee, *Oral Reading of the Scriptures.* Boston: Houghton Mifflin Company, 1974. G. B. Harrison and John McCabe, *Proclaiming the Word.* New York: Pueblo Publishing Company, 1976. Joseph Staudacher, *Laymen Proclaim the Word.* Chicago: Franciscan Herald Press, 1973.

3. There are several such commentaries in print. Jerome Du-Charme has published a popular three volume paperback, *Readers' Guide to Proclamation* (Northport, N.Y.: Costello Publishing Company, 1974) in which each volume covers one cycle of readings. Another substantial volume designed for priests, but suitable for

lectors is *Commentaries on the Readings of the Lectionary* by Robert Crotty, C.P.and Gregory Manly, C.P. (New York: Pueblo Publishing Company, 1975). My own favorite is *Preaching the New Lectionary* by Reginald H. Fuller (Collegeville, Minnesota: The Liturgical Press, 1974).

4. *National Bulletin on Liturgy*. A review published by the Canadian Conference of Bishops, "Training Readers." Ottawa, Ontario: Publications Service, 1976. Volume 9, number 56, November–December, 1976, p. 288.

5. *Ibid.,* pp. 288–289.

6. Eugene A. Walsh, S.S., *Practical Suggestions for Celebrating Sunday Mass.* Old Hickory, Tennessee: Pastoral Arts Association of North America, 1978, p. 52.

7. Clarke, *op. cit.,* p. 52.

8. Hardman, *op. cit.,* pp. 22–23.

9. *Ibid.,* pp. 13–15.

10. Staudacher, *op. cit.,* p. 11.

11. *Ibid.*

12. Hardman, *op. cit.,* p. 12.

13. Staudacher, *op. cit.,* pp. 12–13.

14. *Ibid.,* p. 14.

15. John 15:5.

16. 2 Corinthians 12:7–10.

## CHAPTER 9

1. *Study Text 3, op. cit.,* pp. 20–21.

2. Matthew 16:24.

3. Matthew 5:48.

4. Matthew 26:41.

5. John 13:14–15.

6. *Vatican Council II, op. cit.,* "Decree on the Ministry and Life of Priests," article 12, p. 886.

7. *Order of Mass,* prayer that priest says quietly before the Gospel, if there is no deacon. *Study Text 3, op. cit.,* pp. 51–53.

8. The pattern and format of these reflective periods grew out of the Parish Renewal Experience developed by Father Chuck

Gallagher, S.J., although the context is this author's.

9. Details about this excerpt are taken from the footnotes of the *New American Bible* and from *The Jerome Biblical Commentary* (Englewood Cliffs, N.J.: Prentice-Hall, Inc., 1968), p. 270.

10. A word of thanks here to Jesuit Father Vincent B. McCorry who cited these Old Testament heroes on a retreat given at Auriesville, N.Y. in the summer of 1981.

11. Hebrews 4:15.

12. Hebrews 5:7.

13. This summary and these references are taken from that magnificent treatise on prayer, the *General Instruction of the Liturgy of the Hours* (New York: Catholic Book Publishing Company, 1976), articles 3–4.

14. Hebrews 4:12.

15. John J. Delaney, *Dictionary of Saints*. Garden City, New York: Doubleday, 1980, pp. 311–313.

16. An excerpt from this commentary occurs in the Office of Readings for the memorial celebration of St. Jerome, Priest and Doctor which falls on September 30. *The Liturgy of the Hours*. New York: Catholic Book Publishing Company, 1975, Volume IV, pp. 1447–1449.

17. *Vatican Council II,* "Constitution on the Sacred Liturgy," article 24, p. 10.